THE LIES
I TELL

by

MARLENE A.S. HICKMAN

PUBLISHING

Little Rock

2021

THE LIES
I TELL

A memoir based on my journey that begins in the hills of St. Ann, Jamaica to New York City.

by

MARLENE A.S. HICKMAN

The Lies I Tell

Print ISBN 13: 978-1-949934-51-9
EBook ISBN: 978-1-949934-52-6
Copyright 2021 by Marlene A.S. Hickman

Published by Faith 2 Fe Publishing,
PO Box 242692, Little Rock, AR 72223
www.publishyourfaith.com

CONTENTS

Dedication

This book is dedicated to:

To my friends Jenny and Shawrline, you were a big part of this journey. You supported me in so many ways, such as giving me shelter when I was homeless and feeding me when I was starving. You nurtured me when I went through difficult times and were the family I never had. You were the wings that made me soar when life was kicking my rear.

To Molly Swaby, R.I.P. Twice, you made me angry. But I am so grateful that you chose to be a part of my life. I know you are smiling at me from up above.

To my cousin, Peter Mott, you also found me and made me family. You influenced my decision to attend college and made me realize that writing is possible as I watched you work on your poetry book.

To Leslie Ann, God put a special heart in you to be on my journey and to show me the power of forgiveness, as well as true love and a caring spirit.

To my children, Tiffany and Ocean, there is nothing too hard for you to do. You do your part, and God will do the rest.

To my sister Debbie, it has been a journey of ups and

downs. To you and your children, keep the goals and the dreams alive.

To John Hickman for listening to God and helping me.

To K. Nash for checking on me over the years.

To all the men that have been in my life, you gave me laughter, tears, and an education. You contributed to the person that I am today.

To Barbara Muckle and Andrea Woodstock for always pouring into my visions.

Above all, I thank God for giving me the strength to overcome and for his undeserved blessings, mercy, and favor.

James 1:12 NIV
Blessed is the one who perseveres under trial
because, having stood the test, that person will
receive the crown of life that the Lord has promised
to those who love him.

Acknowledgments

Thank you, Jenny, Shawrline, Glennis, Natalie B., Althea B. who did not listen to her auntie saying, "I am a bad influence," and Camille H. for giving me love.

Thank you, Janet, for believing in me when no one else did. Sorry that life pulled us apart.

Thank you, Peter Mott, and family.

To Carolyn, Suzette, Steve, Andrew, Coleen, and Edgerton, I wish you all the love in the world.

To Leslie, thank you for all you do. God has a place just for you.

Thank you, my sister, Suzette King, for helping me with my vision.

Thank you John Hickman, for always helping us.

Thank you Barbara Muckle and Andrea Woodstock, for your faith in me.

Thank you to my niece, Kizwani Todd, for helping with technical things when I am stuck.

Thank you Katrina Asante and Danisha Anderson. I never forget kindness.

Thank you Natalie Boreland, for returning at the right time.

To all the professional people who treated me like family: Noel Miller, Cheri Taylor, Andrea Woodstock, Barbara Muckle, Fareedah Laney, Gioviandi Singh, Lilyn

Hill, Diana Coleman, Giselle Gavilanes, Shakera, and LeMichele. Thank you, a million times, for your support and encouragement.

To the Reader

Dear Reader,

Thank you for purchasing this book. If you are reading this book, I know that you have your own story.

This story is based on my life. I share the story of my struggles of early childhood abuse, of moving to New York, of being homeless, of making foolish decisions, of my personal struggles of living in New York as an "illegal alien," searching for love, searching for my own space and a journey of hope, faith, and forgiveness.

I hope my struggles will inspire you or someone you know to dream big, to overcome abuse and poverty, and to grow as a person.

This book will reframe how you view your struggles and help you to know that "All is Possible" and when "You Do Your Part, GOD DOES THE REST!"

This book will inspire you to be resilient, to dream big, and to get out of whatever it is that is holding you back, preventing you from moving forward.

Marlene A. S. Hickman

Part One:

Jamaica

Chapter One

My name is Maxine. That was the name I answered to before I started school. That is also the name that people who know me well call me. There are days my heart feels so broken that I force myself to do things. My heart has been feeling broken for an exceedingly long time.

The first time my heart was broken, I was ten years old and sitting in the schoolyard of Brown's Town Primary School. The classrooms were part of an open building. Walls were only on one side of the building, and dividers separated the classrooms of each grade. There were no doors and only several white, metallic windows that were always opened to allow the cool breeze in to keep the classrooms cool except on rainy days. The brown wooden desks that we sat on faced the teacher's wooden table in front of the room, while the silver metallic cupboard with the teacher's supplies faced the wooden desks. Ms.

Dacosta, my teacher, had her chalkboard nailed to the wall, and she kept the white chalk on the window ledge.

I was in the 5th grade and was sitting on the floor at the edge of the 4th-grade building, swinging my legs and talking to Claudia, my ten-year-old friend. I watched as the other children jumped rope; their blue and white uniforms intercepted dust from the reddish colored dirt along with their shiny black school shoes that took a light layer of dirt with each jump. A group of sixth-grade girls was sitting on the steps of the 6th-grade building. Some were reading, while one girl braided another girl's hair. The sun's fervent rays beat on the younger children's heads as they played or read in the schoolyard. Children's laughter echoed as they shouted at their friends in playful fun while the cool island breeze caressed their skin and mine as I swung my legs. The melody of various birds' chirpings was loud, while the smell of bulgur rice wafted in the air from the school kitchen where the cooks prepared our lunches.

It was morning time, and we were on recess and being supervised by several of the younger teachers that were talking in the 5th-grade building. However, their eyes stayed alert, and they were quick to yell any child's name that was observed playing roughly with a peer. I was in my favorite place. It gave me a view of the schoolyard with less exposure to the sun's fervent rays.

The headaches worsened when I played in the sun, so as much as I loved to run around the schoolyard with the other children, I felt crippled by headaches that often hurt when I was in the sun for a long time. These headaches were often accompanied by nausea, making it difficult for me to see, as well as making it feel as though I was being hit on my head. Years later, I would learn that my headaches had a name, "migraine." One woman told me my headaches were due to me having a demonic spirit in me.

Claudia whispered, "They lock up Ms. Grace's (one of the teachers') husband fi frig off her daughter." Her short black hair was braided neatly in small braids. Her blue ribbons blowing in the breeze while blue hair bows formed a pattern at the end of each braid. Her dark chocolate skin was shining and moist from the coconut oil that her mother rubbed on it before school, while her dark-colored eyes glistened with the excitement of gossip.

Claudia was the same age as I was, and in the two years since we had become friends, I admired that she was always "in the know." She was often quiet, but when she talked, I listened as she gossiped about the children or adults around me.

Claudia lived in Dumbarton, quite a distance from the school, but her father drove her to school daily in a white car as he headed to his job at Kaiser Bauxite. Claudia's father was of a fair complexion, while her mother was of a much darker complexion. In my childish mind, I often saw Claudia's father as mysterious since he often dropped her off quickly before driving off. I had no concept of what he did at work, so I assumed he was driving off to a place that was far away. It was also one of my first memories of another father's interaction with his daughter. Maybe that is the reason it stayed in my memory.

My heart was beating fast, and my head was feeling heavy. For the first time, I learned that "frig" is the same word that my cousin, Molly, used to describe what the dogs did, and that people did the same. Claudia continued to whisper. I stared at her open-mouthed, but I no longer heard her words. Luckily for me, Claudia did not know my thoughts. I felt numb. I no longer felt like myself. The happy part of me was leaving, and the new me was now sitting next to Claudia. That "me" was sad, of a caramel complexion, with two waist-length jet black curly braids, big brown eyes, and "magwa." (That is a word for "thin" people in Jamaica.)

My ill-fitted, navy-blue tunic uniform hung from my body, covering the white short-sleeved school shirt like a balloon. The uniform was made to grow with me as I grew. Even my black patent shoes with the two buckles across the front were a size larger than my feet. One shoe stayed unbuckled most of the time since I had a hard time buckling it. Some adults called me "Coolie" which was a word that described my appearance—a mixture of Indian, African, Japanese, Korean, and Caucasian (I found out much later). Some children teased me by saying, "Coolie shit pon callaloo," which was a local vegetable that was cultivated in most yards and the word "Coolie" a derogatory name for Indians. I did not like being teased, but I was not one to argue or be assertive with anyone since I was one of the shortest children in the 5th grade.

Claudia's voice interrupted my thoughts, "Yuh mouth full a blood." I stared at her while swallowing the blood from the inside of my cheek where I had bitten into it. The "normal" that I knew was forever shattered that day, and that was the first time my heart was broken.

I lived in a house whose exterior walls were painted

light pink. It had a huge veranda enclosing the front of the house. In comparison to the other houses in Cockpit, it was one of the largest houses in the surrounding neighborhood. The veranda was surrounded by a black metallic gate lined by flowerpots filled with a variety of plants that my father's wife referred to as "Mi flowers dem." I often pretended those flowers were my students when no one was watching me. I taught them just like my teachers taught me and beat them when they "did not listen."

The veranda's large glass panes reflected the surrounding trees that must have confused the local birds at times since there were days that we picked up dead birds off the veranda that had broken their necks from flying in the window. Mango trees, banana trees, avocado trees, orange trees, and other fruit trees flourished in the yard. A sprawling manicured green lawn was in the front of the house surrounded by more carefully selected flowers that could be observed from Uncle Son's bedroom that had one door entrance from the veranda. As a young child, I was always getting beatings for writing on the veranda walls since I spent a lot of time there.

I lived with my father, Uncle Son. He was of a fair complexion, about five feet, six inches tall, with a medium build and green or grey eyes, depending on when you looked at them. Most people call him "Son." I do not know where that name came from. The name "Face Man" was a name he earned (as I would later learn) due to him being considered attractive. I called him "Uncle Son," and that was the name that Molly called him. Uncle Son had jet black, curly hair. He wore gold-rimmed glasses and had two gold teeth in the front of his mouth. He smelled of a car's engine oil and sweaty armpits. His green eyes were always red, and he sneezed and sniffled constantly. Now that I am older, I know that his smell came from him repairing cars. He was an auto mechanic and owned a passenger bus that transported people from Brown's Town to Kingston. He sniffled because he had allergies. The other people in the house were his wife, Ms. Lupin, my oldest sister, Annmarie, who was two years older than I was, a stepchild, two younger siblings, and the youngest brother, who was born much later when I was a teenager.

Annmarie and I shared a bedroom and shared a bed until I was about six years old. Our bedroom was at the back of the house, at the end of a long corridor. My bed was to the left of the bedroom door, below the glass windows, while Annmarie's bed was at the opposite end under the brown louvre windows. Our shared dresser was to the right of the bedroom's entrance, and it held our few items of clothing folded neatly in the dresser drawers. At the corner of the bedroom door, stood a white wooden bookshelf supported by three legs with some textbooks on the shelves. A brown wooden rocking chair was in the middle of both beds. Its chipped legs reflected the times we spent rocking in the chair as hard as we could. The bedroom door stayed open at times as we were never allowed to close or lock the door at Uncle Son's command.

When I shared a bed with Annmarie, there were many mornings I woke up in urine and got beatings from Uncle Son for "pissing up the bed." I often wondered how I urinated on the bed, and my underwear stayed dry. However, since they were telling me I was "pissing the bed," I believed. Uncle Son and Ms. Lupin would be angry with me each morning that I woke up in urine and often threatened me about having to sleep outside since I could not be trusted to sleep in a bed. But that did not prevent me from waking up in urine.

One night, Uncle Son and Ms. Lupin sent me to sleep outside in the yard because I had "pissed the bed." It was a moonless night as I sat on the steps in the backyard dressed in my pajamas. All the lights were turned off in the house, the sounds of crickets and an owl's cries reminded me of all the "Duppy" the local word for ghost stories that were common among the children and adults. I worried about a "Duppy" coming as I grew more scared by the seconds.

I was exhausted, but fear kept me awake. As my eyes got accustomed to the dark, I saw a black figure hopping towards me that I believed to be "Jimbas—the Boogey Man who took away bad children." I screamed, "Stick him, Jumbie," to our brown dog while I picked up small stones and threw them at "Jimbas," who hopped away while Jumbie was barking at him. Uncle Son and Ms. Lupin then opened the door and asked, "Wha happen to yuh?" I was crying hysterically and was unable to tell them that I had seen Jimbas. It was a frightful experience for me, and it was expected to cure me from "pissing the bed." However, I continued to wake up in urine daily until Annmarie and I were given our own twin beds to protect her from my urine. My bed was always dry, but Annmarie's bed was often urine-soaked. It was not until I became a teenager that it occurred to me that Annmarie had been putting me in her urine while I slept at night.

Annmarie was of a darker complexion than I was. Her hair was short, coarse, and a natural brown color, and she had dark eyes. She was medium-framed and stronger than I was, and she terrorized me for most of my childhood by hitting me, pinching me, and sometimes beating me as she said, "Dem love you because you have long hair. When mi done with you, dem won't love you."

I often wished my appearance were more like Annmarie in my childhood. Then, I would not have to listen to Uncle Son's sister, Diane, talk about me being a "jacket," a word used to describe me not being his child. I concluded that it was also the reason that she always treated Annmarie nicely while she ignored me. My paternal grandmother, Ms. Ivy, also gave me sad stares when Diane talked about me being a "jacket." As I got older, I also concluded that it was the reason that Uncle Son looked at me with hatred and treated me differently than the other children in the home. When I had issues with Annmarie, he often addressed my behaviors by saying, "Hey gal, Maxine, how you mean to _____ my daughter Annmarie?" That made me feel that he was saying Annmarie was his daughter, and I was not. As a child, I took those thoughts and put them in that place that I had learned to put events that hurt or did not make sense.

Growing up, I often listened at nights as Annmarie gave Uncle Son reports on all events in the home during his daily absence, including any rules that I had broken. Sometimes her reports resulted in Uncle Son beating me or having arguments with Ms. Lupin. Each year, it bothered me when Uncle Son gave Annmarie birthday presents while he ignored my birthdays. In addition to treating Annmarie better than any of the other children in the home, Uncle Son showed preferential treatment to Annmarie by giving her everything she asked for. At times, I would make bargains with Annmarie to ask him for things that I wanted so that she could share with me. I disliked Annmarie because her mean disposition and behaviors were directed to everyone else in the home, except Uncle Son.

Once, as Uncle Son and Ms. Lupin argued, Annmarie brought the machete to Uncle Son for him to kill Ms. Lupin. There was also an incident where I asked Annmarie to braid my then waist-length hair, which she did, and then laughed as she watched me struggle to unbraid it, creating tangles that made it painful to comb through. I benefitted from her mean disposition only in school because the other children did not mess with me. Later in adulthood, I learned to look beyond Annmarie's faults by maintaining a relationship with her despite the other siblings and Ms. Lupin shunning her.

I owned two pairs of shoes at any given time during my childhood, one pair of shoes to wear to school and the other to wear to church or to the market. I hated my Hush Puppies school shoes. They were often a size larger than my feet. Since they never got damaged, I often wore the same shoes for about two years to school without them having to be replaced. My friends often compared my old shoes to their nice new ones, so I learned, as I got older, to cut the threads with a razor so the shoes would get damaged to get a new pair of shoes at the beginning of each school year.

I owned less than ten pieces of clothing during my

childhood, not including my school uniforms, and I never questioned the reasons I had only a few pieces of clothing. I learned early that instead of buying store-bought clothes, Ms. Lupin would make my dresses. As a result, I never owned pretty clothes as my friends did. One year, when I wore a dress that she made to the Annual High School Fair, my friend, Claudille, told me that her brother Seymour told her I "wore a crocus bag to the school fair." (A crocus bag was the course brown bag that sugar came in.)

I awoke daily around six a.m. to the sound of Uncle Son's voice, yelling, "Maxine, get up, gal." My eyes opened to the large ackee tree's limbs hanging outside the bedroom window. Ackee continues to be my favorite food, but I grew to hate the tree since it reminded me daily that I was in Uncle Son's house.

Some nights, I escaped in my dreams to my mother Dahlia's house, whom I met when I was six years old, or to places that existed only in dreams. I was told that Dahlia had dropped me off to Uncle Son's mother, Ms. Ivy, at the house she shared with his sister, Diane, in Orange Hill, when I was two years old. They say that at two years old, children do not have memories. But I remembered standing on the veranda and looking in the direction of where Dahlia had disappeared.

I lived with Diane and Ms. Ivy until Uncle Son's marriage to Ms. Lupin when I was four years old. Then, I was sent to live with Ms. Lupin, Annmarie, and Uncle Son. Each morning, I performed my chores of feeding the chickens in the yard and making breakfast for Uncle Son before getting ready for school. I resented that Annmarie could sleep late while I was expected to wake up early.

Ms. Lupin also slept late; her snoring was often heard all the way in the dining room from her bedroom that was in the back of the house. I often imagined her snores shaking the picture frames of flowers off the living room wall. I despised Ms. Lupin's locked door, but I was only a child and never allowed to express any thoughts or feelings.

Ms. Lupin was taller than Uncle Son. She was about 5 feet, 10 inches, with a dark complexion and slender-framed. She had short black hair that she wore in a relaxer, and she had an acne-scarred face. Thick unruly eyebrows framed Ms. Lupin's dark eyes, and when she laughed, it was a guttural sound. Ms. Lupin was enrolled in Teacher's College for most of my early childhood, and I loved to read her textbooks. Her textbooks often covered the wooden dining room table that was only cleared for visitors while we ate at the aluminum dinner table. I viewed Ms. Lupin as the mother in the house, addressed her as "Ms. Lupin," and never spent much time thinking about our relationship. Ms. Lupin loved listening to gospel music on her 45 records and LPs, which she played loudly on the stereo in the living room.

On her bad days, which seemed to be the days she did the laundry (she would hand wash the clothes), she cursed about having to "...wash the gal dem clothes," referring to Ann Marie and me. On the days that she had to clean the floors in the house, she cursed about having to clean the floor, saying, "...while the two-gal dem do nothing," followed by her humming and singing her gospel song of choice for that day. As a result, Annmarie and I started crawling on our knees to wipe the black-and-white-tiled floor with rags because she said the floor did not get clean with a mop. We also hand washed our clothes by the time I was six years old. As we got older, Annmarie and I learned to pull the younger children in blankets on the floor to give the floor a sheen without having to shine it while on our knees.

On her good days, Ms. Lupin monitored my schoolwork, corrected my grammatical errors, and talked to me. She taught me new vocabulary as she learned them and encouraged my love for reading. Ms. Lupin taught me that I should never have to beg any man that I am with for money. She said, "A man should know you need soap to wash your rear," and "Never wear no panties with holes in them." She said that so many times that I am now forced to throw out any underwear that I own with holes in them. "Always make your bed, in case you faint outside, and someone have to bring you home." As a result, I make my bed as soon as I wake up in the mornings. Sometimes she responded, "You will see..." to the numerous questions that always flowed through my mind.

Ms. Lupin appeared to enjoy sitting for long periods on the veranda, squeezing the acne on her face. When she talked to anyone, she was always quick to say, "Me and my two pickney dem," and later, when she gave birth to the last one, "Me and my three pickney dem." Those phrases contributed to making me feel that I never belonged there. Throughout my childhood, Ms. Lupin never attended or participated in any events that related to Annmarie and me, so I viewed her as having a separate life from us. Uncle Son and Ms. Lupin never showed public affection; however, they were unanimous in telling Annmarie and me, "You won't come off to nothing, you good fi nothing gals."

Ms. Lupin described herself as, "Me a good Christian woman." She was raised in the Seventh Day Adventist Church and attended church on Saturdays. Sometimes I attended church with her and enjoyed eating with her family after church. On the Saturdays that I did not accompany her to church, we had to wait for her to return home to cook us soup extremely late on Saturday nights. For years after I left home, I refused to eat soup.

Uncle Son proudly attended the Baptist Church in Brown's Town on holiday Sundays only and did not speak much about God or religion. I learned about God and Jesus from church, school, and from Judy, one of the young girls from Cockpit who was a member of the Jehovah's Witnesses church. Judy enjoyed teaching me Bible stories from the colorful Jehovah's Witnesses Children's Bible. Those events were my introduction to religion and developed my curiosity of God and a fascination with Bible stories. My favorite Bible stories were the ones about Creation and the ones that told of God's wrath and punishment.

I was taught that the Bible teaches hope, love, forgiveness, faith, and of the end of life on earth. I embraced those teachings in my life and took them literally. I hoped and waited for God to strike Uncle Son dead as He had done to the firstborn Egyptian children in Exodus 11:4. Whenever Uncle Son was late coming home, I prayed and thanked God for killing him and would be so disappointed when he eventually showed up. I enjoyed reading the book of Revelation as I imagined the destruction it would cause on earth and of Uncle Son's judgment. I remained hopeful throughout my childhood that the world would end quickly so that my abuse would end. Later, in my adult years, I utilized other Bible books and their teachings along with the concept of faith and hope to bring me through dark periods in my life and decreased my focus on the book of Revelation.

Annmarie and I were expected to perform all the household chores while Uncle Son and Ms. Lupin monitored our work to ensure everything was done the way they liked. For many years, we used to get beatings for not cleaning the bathroom properly, even though we cleaned the bathtub, sink, toilet bowl, and repeatedly mopped the floor. We later discovered that Uncle Son had been putting dead roaches behind the bathroom door. Since we kept the bathroom door open while cleaning it, we would never sweep behind the door. Uncle Son would beat Annmarie and me for any task that we did not do "properly" or for any task "Yuh did not do." He used any item he found available to hit us with, and at some point, in our early childhood, he started hitting us with an old leather fan belt from the car. He was not selective with the body part the fan belt hit, which resulted in Annmarie and me having cuts and welts all over our bodies. But in a community that encouraged physical punishment, no one really cared.

As we got older, Annmarie refused to assist with most of the household chores, while Uncle Son said nothing. Ms. Lupin ignored her after the incident with the machete as well as other negative behaviors that Annmarie directed towards her and her children. I found that I was doing most of the chores, and by the time I became a teenager, the neighbors teased me by calling me "Cinderella." I did not mind sweeping, mopping, dusting, cooking for the family, and making up the beds for Uncle Son, Ms. Lupin, and the other children daily. I would also supervise the younger children's baths. Fortunately, I did not have to wash their clothes because a washerwoman would come in weekly to wash their clothes. The more I cleaned, the more I appreciated organization and the feeling of clean.

Annmarie and I were always told, "Go do some work, gal," when Ms. Lupin or Uncle Son observed us playing. So, we learned to sneak to the neighbors' yard adjacent to the house to play with Charmaine and Colleen when they were not home. We built homes made of coconut palm leaves and baked cakes made of the red dirt while we pretended to travel to America via airplanes by climbing the fruit trees. I was the best climber among the group and climbed the fruit trees while throwing fruits down to the others.

Luckily for us, Charmaine and Colleen's mother, Ms. Dan, and their grandmother, Ms. Ethlyn, knew we were not allowed to play. So, they often warned us to go home when Uncle Son's vehicles were heard coming down the hill. Annmarie and I mastered running home quickly and sitting on the steps to the veranda while the vehicle slowly descended the hill to await their arrival home. Ms. Dan was the one who sneaked us both to watch the funeral procession of the legendary singer Bob Marley as he traveled through Brown's Town to his final resting place in the hills of St. Ann in May, 1981.

As a young child, my one pleasure was reading because

I found escape in the adventures that were present in books. I made weekly trips to the Brown's Town Library and borrowed books, as well as enjoyed reading the dictionary. I also excelled academically at Brown's Town Primary. In a school system that placed children based on overall grades, I was mostly child number one in overall grades or child number two in mathematics a few times in the five years that I was a student there.

I loved three teachers at Brown's Town Primary School. I loved Ms. Swaby, my second-grade teacher, for the praises she gave to my essays. As an adult, I would learn that my cousin Molly was Ms. Swaby's husband's daughter and made me realize that was the reason Ms. Swaby often asked me about Molly and Diane. I loved Ms. Dacosta, my fifth-grade teacher, for forcing me to pay attention in class by putting me to sit with the boys when I would lose focus by talking to the girls and Ms. Johnson, my sixth-grade teacher, for believing in me and refusing to accept mediocre classwork from me. It was at Brown's Town Primary that I entered my first speech competitions where I won a Bronze Medal in the National School's Competition as well as was the second runner up in my school's competition for the spelling bee representative.

I looked forward to Christmas because the teachers assigned us roles in the Christmas story. I was often assigned the role of an angel. I found it exciting to participate in such a powerful story and loved that after the show we were given small presents. It was unimportant that the presents were often items such as pencils, coloring books, or puzzle books. It was a thrill to pull the wrapping paper off and discover the secret. At

Christmas, Uncle Son purchased a real pine tree that he would place in the corner of the veranda where Annmarie and I would proudly decorate the tree with balloons and the handmade decorations that we had made. The tree was more symbolic of Christmas since we were never given presents. The best thing that happened on Christmas morning was that our grand-uncle, Mr. Miller, always visited us, along with our great grand-aunt, Ms. Gwen, who gave us money annually.

Chapter Two

I may not have fit the "typical image" of a child that was being abused. The family appeared to be "well," and we lived in a nice house that Uncle Son had designed and built. Uncle Son and Ms. Lupin drove nice cars, and we were always clean and well-groomed. There were days that Ms. Lupin refused to give us food, but since we ate lunch in school, we survived those times. As I got older and the abuse continued, I started thinking it was my fault. I no longer smiled a lot when I was at home, and I wore long dresses to cover my body. I felt that by covering myself, the abuse would stop, and when Ms. Lupin told me to cut my long hair when I was ten years old because it was unmanageable, I did as she instructed. I was hopeful that any change to my outer appearance would stop the abuse.

Molly often visited us and spent nights at our home. On one of her visits, Molly, who knew of the abuse, told us to tell Ms. Lupin of the abuse. Molly decided that I should be the one to tell Ms. Lupin since I was the youngest and would be listened to. I told Ms. Lupin, and she stared at me and was silent. That night, I was awakened as Uncle Son grabbed me by my hair and pulled me out of bed and gave me one of the worse beatings you could imagine with a green water hose to my head. Molly was apologetic to me after that incident and rarely visited us after that. That beating built the fear and secrecy in me that it was intended to do.

I knew to never speak of my abuse to anyone except for my doll. I acted out the behaviors as I played with her. My doll was nameless, but I played with her as often as I could. Her long blonde hair was matted, and it did little in covering her ivory-colored nude body that was decorated with dog bites, while her one leg dangled in the left direction. I used to beat the doll in the ways Uncle Son beat me, and I twisted her leg when I felt frustrated. As children, we were only provided an item once, and it was understood that those items would be cared for and never be replaced. So, that was the only doll I ever owned in my childhood.

As I got older, I used to run away when I knew he wanted to beat me. One Sunday evening, I knew Uncle Son was going to beat me, so I decided to run away and go to my Uncle Boss's house in Orange Hill. As I walked up the hill to his house, Uncle Son's car stopped alongside me. I was crippled with fear as he immediately grabbed me by my hair, wrapped it around his hand, and threw me into the back of the car. He punched me several times in my head with his fists while I cowered on the floor and urinated on myself. After that incident, Uncle Son started to wait for me to go to bed at night before hitting me in my sleep. I awoke to the fan belt's stings across my arms so many times that I began to cover my face during my sleep. I still sleep with my arms covering my face today.

At 11 years old, I passed the Common Entrance Examination (the examination given to enter High School), and I started Westwood High School in September 1980. Nestled in the hills of Trelawny, the school boasts of "turning girls into proper young ladies" and was considered one of the best girls' boarding schools in Jamaica. I viewed school as an escape from home and must have been one of the few girls who hated when school was on breaks.

I did well academically in the seventh grade and the beginning of the eighth grade. However, as I read more and learned more, I was influenced by American Literature that described children utilizing behaviors as messages. I decided to fail academically in the final semester of eighth grade and in the ninth grade as a deliberate cry for help. My intention was for the school's guidance counselor to notice my failing grades and to conclude that I was being abused.

It took two years of failing classes and of my favorite teachers embarrassing me by saying, "I don't know what is wrong with you, but you need to get it together," for me to understand that no one would talk to me about abuse. So, I started doing my schoolwork again in the ninth grade with a goal to "just pass," since I no longer cared.

My best friends in seventh, eighth, and ninth grade were Natalie B. and Shernette D. Somehow, my relationship terminated with Shernette D. after the eighth-grade school fair, and I assumed it had something to do with another student who spent a lot of time whispering. Natalie B. was allowed to visit my home, and I could visit her home in Sturge Town because Ms. Lupin used to rent a room from her family when she taught at the local school in Sturge Town. Natalie B. and I shared July birthdays and shared many things in common. Natalie B. and I talked about mostly everything, except for the secret of abuse that I carried. However, as we entered the ninth grade, we drifted apart and started interacting with other girls.

Back then, most of us from Westwood High School liked boys that attended York Castle High School. My "boy likes" were Silbourne, Claudille's brother in the seventh grade, who sent me a bottle of Charlie perfume and a mixed tape, and in the eighth grade, it was Richie from Mamee Bay. They were both break dancers. Later, it was Michael C. with the green eyes in the tenth grade.

In the tenth grade, strangers, both men, and women began telling me I was beautiful, but I never saw myself as beautiful. Women commented on my long eyelashes so I used to trim them with scissors so that I would not be noticed. Secrets, pain, shame, and the guilt of abuse stared back at me when I looked in the mirror. I felt like a sponge, absorbing everything around me, yet nothing left. Quite often, I felt devoid of emotions and detached as every waking moment greeted me with my secret. It was difficult to cry although I was hurting, and my tears no longer flowed during Uncle Son's beatings, which he viewed as defiance and would say, "Yuh think yuh a woman, gal?" He hit me harder and longer.

In the tenth grade, some of the other girls formed a

group called the *Khrazy Kidz*. I became a member of the group because I was friendly with most of the girls. It felt good to belong to a "group," and it gave me a sense of belonging. We spent a lot of time sitting under the grapevines outside the school's main office, gossiping and talking. Some of the girls talked about their families and their lives outside of school, while I was careful not to talk about my life.

Since it was the 1980s, we spent time learning all the words of the popular songs and were captivated by Michael Jackson like the rest of the world. Camille D. even had a Michael Jackson's *Thriller* jacket and lent it to me. We also spent time reading *Right On, Jet*, and *Ebony Magazine*, as well as *Harlequin Mills* and *Boone* romance books, *Nancy Drew*, and *The Hardy Boys* books. Those books would be read and passed on to each girl that was interested in them.

I also participated in the drama and the debate clubs. Two highlights of this period were to enter the All-High-School Drama Club Festival playing alongside Yolande B. and winning a certificate of mention. I listened to my friend's encouragement and entered the school's annual Ms. Westwood High School competition. I won the title of the Most Intelligent Contestant, but I already knew that I would not have won the Miss Westwood title because I did not own nice clothes. Celeste L. won, wearing one of her beautiful dresses as always. My best memory of that day was of Delky Wood's big hugs as she congratulated me before she succumbed to an episode of seizure seconds from her congratulations. I remembered Delky often talked about combing her hair nightly because she wanted to have nice hair if she woke up in heaven. Now, as I write, I know that Delky is smiling in heaven with neatly combed hair.

At the end of the summer of 1985, and Ms. Lupe's return from her annual Florida trip, I decided to run away from the house with my sister, Annmarie. We left at night while everyone was asleep, and we walked the dark street aimlessly due to poor planning. As we walked, a young man we knew recognized us in the dark and told us to come with him. We knew we would be safe with him, so we went to his house at Top Roads, and he allowed us to sleep there.

While at the young man's home, I decided to travel to St. Catherine to go and live with my mother Dahlia. Our friends Sherman, Mark, and Michael C. picked us up from the young man's home and drove me to get on the bus to travel to my mother. Mark and Michael C. were friends and often met up with us due to Mark being in a relationship with one of my close friends at the time. Michael C. and I kissed several times.

I arrived at Dahlia's house in Content District, St. Catherine, hopeful about a future of living with her and her other children. It was during that visit that I noticed the poverty that Dahlia lived in, which Uncle Son always talked about. Dahlia was supported by her younger children's father. Dahlia was shorter than me and wore her short hair in small curls.

I inherited her shiny face, her thick calves, and her soft-spoken voice that ended in a shriek when she yelled. Dahlia had given birth to her first child, Edgie, when she was fifteen years old and had me when she was seventeen years old. She always wore a smile, and I often wondered what her view of life was since that smile stayed stuck on her face. Dahlia, her man, and their children lived in a bright blue, two-bedroom house with an outside kitchen, an outside toilet away from the house, and an enclosed zinc area for bathing. Fruit trees surrounded the yard, and the dirt yard was always swept clean by my brothers.

Dahlia hand washed clothes daily in a large aluminum pan that she placed under a large tree without complaints while listening to the radio. She spent the evenings doing crossword puzzles from the daily newspaper sitting under the same tree. Dahlia appeared happy, despite her surroundings. She never talked about things she did not have or about dreams or goals.

I often thought that her dreams and goals were in her children since she was observed to care for her man and those children in all her waking moments. Dahlia was usually awake at the first cock's crow and stayed outside at night with Clydie while he smoked cigarettes or marijuana spliffs before going to bed.

I welcomed Dahlia's living conditions as I shared a bedroom with my three younger sisters and two brothers. My oldest brother, Edgie, had been kicked out of the house years before on one of my previous visits. My sisters and I slept on one bed, and my two younger brothers slept next to us on their bed.

I told Dahlia about the abuse and I told her I did not want to return to Uncle Son's house but wanted to attend St. Catherine High School with my sister, Car. Dahlia remained quiet, which I thought strange at the time. I thought she agreed with me staying with her and enrolling in St. Catherine High School, which I did and attended school for one week in September of 1985.

That same week, Dahlia sent me to her brother P's house in Portmore, where he lived with his wife D. and his daughter R. with a letter. P. was a police detective and was considered as doing "well" in my maternal family. I assumed P. and Dahlia decided I should return to Uncle Son's house in the letter I was given to return to Dahlia.

On the Sunday after that visit, Dahlia and Uncle Son showed up at my maternal grandmother's house in Kitson Town, where I had gone for the day with my siblings and their male cousins Elvis, Gayon, Horace, and Kirk to pick me up to transport me back to his house. For the first time, I expressed my feelings to Uncle Son. "If you take me back, me a go kill myself," I muttered.

They both ignored me as I reluctantly got in Uncle Son's vehicle for the long ride back to Brown's Town. In the car, I felt rejected and totally disconnected from Dahlia and life. I did not understand Dahlia's decision to send me back to an abusive environment. That began my general distrust towards all the family and the people around me and caused a permanent numbness of my emotions.

The next day I returned to Westwood High School, and my friends welcomed me back. "Where were you?" they asked.

"I went to live with my mother in St. Catherine," I answered.

I was thankful that none of my friends asked my reason for returning to school. Shallo and I then realized that both our mothers lived in St. Catherine, that we both lived with our fathers and a stepmother, and that led us to feel very connected to each other. Shallo was dark-skinned and slender framed with short hair that she relaxed. Shallo had a birth mole on her straight nose, and she had beautiful white teeth. Her breasts were larger than most of us, and they strained against her school uniform when she spoke.

She was voracious and outgoing, while my personality was laid back. I did not like the spotlight and preferred to be an observer, unlike Shallo, who loved the spotlight. I nicknamed her "Ms. Nuffus" in my thoughts since she always forced herself into everything that was being planned in the school. Shallo had been Annmarie's friend when they were in the same grade but later became one of my best friends. Our common attributes changed my view of her, and we became closer. At that time, I did not realize that was the beginning of a lifetime friendship.

I still do not know how I focused on schoolwork that year because by then, many of the local people had heard that I ran away and speculated that, "She run away because her father wants to deh with her." As the rumors circulated, Ms. Lupin did damage control by telling anyone that would listen to her that, "The gal tell lie about her father wanting to deh with her, because she wants to be with men, and he don't allow her."

Uncle Son, Ms. Lupin, and one of her sisters that was staying at the home at the time ignored my presence in the home for several months. Uncle Son punished me for running away by refusing to pay my school fees as well as my CXE examination fees. The fees were only paid after Ms. Logan sent me home from school around

October of 1985 for the money. To avoid embarrassment, Ms. Lupin paid the fees, and Uncle Son reimbursed her. Remembering that time, I realize that I "spaced." I would later learn that abused children either space out or become hypervigilant because they learn to cope with abuse through disassociation. I often felt that I was living life as an observer and was able to separate from anything unpleasant, including the abuse.

At the close of 1985, my close friends were Jackie H., Claudille S., Camille H., Shallo, and Maffe. Unbeknownst to us at that time, some of those relationships would extend beyond high school and Jamaica. 1986 was a historic year for the world. The year opened with the Space Challenger explosion, which the entire school listened to on the radio. That year concluded the last semester of my high school years, and I was elated to be one of the students selected to graduate in the June 1986 Commencement Service since attendance at the commencement services was a privilege.

Graduation selection was made by a graduation committee made up of the school's teachers and some students who viewed academic records, as well as a student's deportment as eligibility for a student to attend the commencement service. As Westwood High School girls, we were also considered to represent the school outside of the school. Unfortunately, "talking to boys" was not "good conduct of young ladies," and I think that resulted in some of my friends not being allowed to graduate. My last report card had good comments except for "Marlene has no tact."

My favorite teachers at Westwood were Ms.

Robinson, my Spanish teacher, Ms. Lawson, my Social Studies teacher, Ms. Wiles, my Home Economics teacher, and my male History teacher, who fathered one of our peer's child shortly after her graduation. Also included were Ms. Walters, my seventh-grade homeroom teacher, who always told me to go comb my hair, Ms. Logan, my assistant principal who never lost her composure, and my math teacher, Mr. Campbell, who made me hate math because I would hear him muttering Jamaican curse words when I repeatedly asked him to explain the math problem.

The principal, Ms. Whiteman, also made an impression in my life as she was always well-dressed and spoke softly to us. In the tenth grade, I had my first contact with a male, white social worker who was my Social Studies teacher from the Peace Corps. He talked about the profession of social work and its goal to help others. The idea of helping people interested me, but my dream at that time was to become a lawyer.

The months after my high school graduation sealed my fate and future. Ms. Lupin left for Florida from June to December 1986, which gave Uncle Son freedom to do as he pleased in the home. He hired a driver to drive his passenger bus while he stayed home and only returned to driving the bus when he realized there was a discrepancy with the money.

During the time he was home, I was only allowed to leave the house to run errands such as grocery shopping, going to the Post Office, or doing his banking. My friends Shallo, Camille H., Althea B., and Maffi visited me when they could and became my sunshine on those days. They had no idea what I was going through since

I was genuinely happy when I saw them. That summer, I asked Uncle Son's permission to enroll in classes at the University of the West Indies to begin a path to law school, and he responded, "Mi nah spend mi money on yuh, and another man come reap it. Yuh think you betta than mi, gal?"

That statement made me realize that if I stayed in the home, I would not have a future or control over my life. I hated him even more for trying to control me, and I started thinking of hurting him or myself if he ever touched me again. God was watching over me because from the time those thoughts became my obsession, Uncle Son left me alone. That July, I celebrated my seventeenth birthday and prayed to God for a miracle in my life by removing me and putting me in America. I figured America was "far away from home" and out of Uncle Son's reach.

That summer, I saw a fallen star for the first time and made a wish to be in America. I also developed a relationship with an adult woman named J., who was in her twenties and lived at the top of the street that led to our house. J. was tall, slender-framed, of a fair complexion, and had bleached blonde hair. J's husband was a detective, and she had three sons.

She was self-employed as a hairdresser out of her garage. I would often talk to her as I walked by her house on my way home. She was easy to talk to and offered empathy when she saw the bruises on my body from Uncle Son's beatings, which other people chose to ignore. J. was the first adult who asked me the reason that Uncle Son did not allow us to socialize with other people. Initially, I was too ashamed to tell J. the truth.

However, once I realized that I would not be headed to law school, I felt hopeless and asked J. to help me leave. J. repeatedly asked my reasons for wanting to leave and never gave up on her probing. So, one day after she said, "Mi know you do not want to tell me, but I will not tell anyone, is it because Uncle Son messing with you, you want to leave? I nodded, yes. "Lord, Jesus, what a wicked man. And him wife know and do nothing, what a wicked woman?" J muttered.

I did not answer, I had just told someone my most terrible secret, and I was worried about her thoughts of me. I looked at her, and I saw what I perceived to be genuine concern and shock in her expression. "Mi wi help you. Mi can tek whatever happens." J. told me. I knew J. was different from other adults I knew, and I felt confident she would help me.

Part Two:

New York

Chapter Three

My new life started Monday, February 23, 1987. Ms. Lupin had taken me to the United States Embassy and applied for a tourist visa for me around January of 1987. I viewed that as God's answer to my prayers, and I started planning my grand escape. I asked J. to help me with purchasing the plane ticket to leave. J. was concerned about me traveling so far away from Jamaica, but I convinced her that I planned to travel to New York and ask Buku's mother if I could stay with her. I picked New York because it was much further away from Florida, where Uncle Son and Ms. Lupin visited when they traveled to the United States.

The night I left, I waited for everyone to fall asleep. I packed my best clothes in a small bag along with my photo album, my high school record, birth certificate, and the greeting cards my friends had given me over the years. Annmarie accompanied me.

As we walked slowly across the backyard, the moon's

dazzling light made it unsafe for us to walk out the front gate because we risked being seen by Uncle Son if he looked out the window. We had to walk across the vacant land next to our house and hoped no one in the house would awake from the dogs barking. One of the dogs followed us and walked with us all the way to J's house. Years later, Annmarie told me the dog never returned home.

Peasy, another male that we knew, offered to drive me to the airport, and he spent the night at J.'s house. Peasy's car windows were darkly tinted, so I knew no one would see us in his car as we drove through Brown's Town to the airport. At the airport, I hugged Annmarie, Camille H., and J. goodbye, not knowing if we would ever see each other again.

My first plane ride was uneventful as I sat next to a young man who talked about returning from spring break in Jamaica and about his parents owning a laundromat. I asked about spring break, and the young man explained it as a school vacation. I listened politely since I did not know what a laundromat was.

On exiting the airplane at JFK airport, I felt the coldest wind I had ever felt in all my 17 years on earth. I did not know that I had picked one of the coldest months to run away to New York. I was wearing a fuchsia-pink, knee-length skirt and matching top. My height of five feet, three inches, was lengthened by another inch from the black pumps I was wearing, and my weight was 95 pounds. My curly black hair was held in place by Vaseline, and my lips glistened with pink lip gloss. My clothes were appropriate for the Jamaican weather but not the New York weather. In my pocketbook, I had a piece of paper with telephone numbers written on it, a $20.00 bill, and some loose coins that Peasy had given me for telephone calls and with the advice of, "Don't get caught up in America." Peasy had also given me the telephone number for his friend Fonzo whom I had met once in Jamaica.

I must have appeared more confident than I felt because when the immigration officer asked, "What is the purpose of your visit?"

"To visit family. I am on spring break," I responded with confidence.

I was grateful that the immigration officer was unaware that schools in Jamaica did not have spring break in February. The immigration officer stamped "six months" in my passport, as I said a silent prayer, thanking God. I walked away from the immigration officer, fearing that he would call me back.

I saw a telephone booth and got the telephone numbers from my pocketbook. I first dialed Buku's mother. I was confident that she would take me in. After all, I had been taking Camille H., home to my house for the past several years from school.

"Hello," a woman's voice answered the telephone.

"This is Maxine, Buku's friend," I said.

"Mi tell her, no one can't stay yah," she said and disconnected the phone. I did not have time to process her answer as I immediately dialed the next number on my list. It was Fonzo's telephone number, and the phone rang several times without an answer.

I looked around at the people waiting around me, and they were all were wearing thick coats as I had seen in movies. I had never worn a coat before, but I imagined that it must be warm because I was the only one that was shivering.

At that moment, I felt I had no choice but to call J.'s friend, Jeff, whom she had introduced to me the past summer when he was on a visit to Jamaica. I called the telephone number, and a woman answered in a professional manner. That was when I realized it was his workplace. "May I speak to Jeff?' I asked.

"What is your name?' she asked.

"Maxine," I answered.

"Jeff is on his way to pick you up," she said.

I knew J. must have called and told him to pick me up from the airport. I did not know what to think. All I knew was that I was in New York and did not have a place to sleep. I did not have to wait long for Jeff's arrival. I saw him as he approached. Jeff was of medium complexion, thick eyebrows, and slender build, and smiled at me as he approached, extending his arms to hug me. I let him hug me but did not extend my arms. This kind of greeting was new to me, and I was uncomfortable with men touching me.

"J. called me and asked me to pick you up," he said, smiling.

"Thank you," I said, as he glanced at my small traveling bag.

"Let us go," he said.

I followed him, not knowing where he was taking me. As always, I was devoid of emotions and felt spaced out.

Outside was even colder than the inside of the airport. The air smelled like ice, and I saw ice on the ground. There had been a snowstorm earlier that day, and piles of snow were everywhere. I had never seen snow before and wished I could touch it.

"Be careful that you don't fall. You're not wearing the right shoes," Jeff said.

Jeff approached a car that had "Yellow Cab" written on it, and he told me we were on our way to Brooklyn. Jeff gave me his winter coat, which I was grateful to have. I stared at the tall buildings as we drove by them, thinking *This is not the America that was shown on television in Jamaica*. On television, the American houses were on tree-lined streets with enclosed fences and looked beautiful. Huge brown and beige buildings skyscrapers were sprawled everywhere, and there were bright lights far off in the horizon. I could not help thinking that the buildings looked like boxes stacked on each other, and everything looked strange to me.

"Oh, by the way, you need to say you are my cousin," Jeff said. I stared at him questioningly. "I tell Lea that you are my cousin," he said.

"Lea?" I asked.

"The girl I live with," he said. "Its business," Jeff explained.

"Okay," I replied. I had heard the term "business" used before. It was a term used to refer to marriages for the purpose of getting one's green card in America or Canada. Several years later, I would meet the woman's cousin Jeff had married for his green card. It was not Lea, as he made me believe. Jeff appeared anxious, but I was not mature enough to ask his reason for looking anxious.

We arrived at their apartment, and Lea greeted me, "How was the flight?'

I responded, "Okay."

"What side of Jeff's family are you on?" she asked.

Jeff answered quickly, "Bongo side." It was the name his father was known by.

I nodded my head. I hoped she would stop asking me about Jeff's family since I had only seen them once and did not know them well.

"Can you cook?" Lea asked.

"Yes," I answered.

"I love Jamaican food," she responded.

They both decided I needed to get a winter coat and boots, and we walked to the Rainbow Store on Flatbush Avenue, where they bought me a blue coat and matching blue boots. As we walked back to the apartment, I observed the surroundings. Restaurants and stores lined the streets while traffic lights indicated when it was safe to cross the street. I had never seen traffic lights before or walk signs, so I was excited to see them. Their apartment building was at the corner of Dorchester Avenue and East 21 Street, which was close to the remarkably busy shopping area.

That night, I was given a bed on the living room sofa. During the night, I dreamed, and my dream was filled with images of Uncle Son molesting me. I was scared and frightened because there was no one to help me. He was chasing me, and as he reached over to grab me, I woke up. That was the beginning of those dreams. My heart was beating rapidly, and I was filled with fear and hate. I opened my eyes, and it took me a few minutes to remember where I was. The ackee tree did not greet me, but windows and curtains. I heard Lea leave for work.

Jeff was also getting ready for work, and I observed him to be moving slowly. I knew he was lingering to speak to me.

"I was shocked when J. called to tell me you were coming," he said.

Jeff and J. had known each other because they were both from the same place in Aboukir. They were also the same age, and their families were friends.

"I did not have anywhere to go. I have Fonzo's telephone number that Peasy gave to me," I told him.

"You should not go to Fonzo. Them people are druggists," he said.

"Oh," I answered.

I had known people that were referred to druggists in Jamaica. That term was used to describe people who were involved in selling marijuana and other illegal substances. Len and his family were known "druggists." I knew Len since I was fourteen years old, and he was eight years older than I was. Len was of a light complexion, light brown eyes, and curly hair. I thought Len was cute, and as I got older, he often offered Annmarie and me car rides when he saw us walking back and forth from our house to Brown's Town. It is common practice in Jamaica to accept car rides. Len drove luxury cars, and I loved cars then and could tell the model of the car by the sound of its engine.

After my graduation in 1986 from high school, Len and I saw more of each other because it became my responsibility to escort my baby brother to and from Brown's Town Infant School. Len would drive by at the same time I escorted my baby brother to school and drive us there. After a while, he started asking me to come with him to his house. Knowing Uncle Son's reputation of not wanting anyone talking to his daughters, Len would tell me, "Look, don't worry about me and your father. I can handle it."

I refused Len's invitation several times, but once Uncle Son refused to pay for me to attend law school, I felt hopeless and isolated. I slept most of the time when I was not doing housework or lying on my bed, spaced out while imagining a different life. I often narrated my life in the third person in my thoughts before going to sleep, which later became a habitual thing for me to do when I was going through difficult times.

I no longer visited the Brown's Town Library because it had become difficult to focus on reading, and I was experiencing an increase in my headaches. I lost interest in everything around me, including food, and I became very thin. Len, I now realized planned and started driving a darkly tinted car as he continued to invite me to his house.

One day, I gave in to his request, and after dropping off my brother at school, I went to his house knowing that I was not visible by anyone from his car. That was also my act of rebellion since I knew Uncle Son would be afraid to confront Len due to his circle. I think that thought also impacted the males that were to be a part of my life for years. At Len's house, I watched movies with him or watched as he cleaned the motorbikes or cars. Len was often quiet; however, he spent a lot of time staring at me and smiling. There were times we cuddled and kissed, but mostly we cuddled. I found peace lying next to him as he ran his fingers through my hair. That touch was my first memory of a comforting touch and peace, and I am still comforted when someone strokes my head today.

One day as he stared at me, he said, "Mi know you a have problems with yuh father. Is he trying to deh with you?"

I looked at Len and started crying. He hugged me as he repeatedly asked me, "Tell me wha wrong?" I refused to answer.

Len's family and friends were viewed as "bad" by many people and my friend Althea B., who lived next door to Len, told me that she was not allowed to "associate with me anymore" because her aunt had seen me at Len's house and now classified me as "a bad influence." Althea B. was then sent away to Kingston to escape my bad influence. I did not care what people thought of me and even when Uncle Son saw Len or any man looking at me his new name for me was "whore or slut." I was numb to the name-calling. I do not know if Len had girlfriends, and although we had kissed many times, he never asked me to have sex with him or touched my private parts.

I felt safe and protected around him, and it became routine for several months for Len to pick me up after I had dropped off my brother at school and take me to his home. One day, I did not see his car, and as I thought of that, one of his friends drove up and told me that he had been stabbed and was in the hospital. I asked the friend if he could take me to the hospital in St. Ann's Bay, which he did.

Len's face was fully bandaged, and it was difficult to see where he had been cut. He had been stabbed across his face. He held my hands as he said, "I don't know you would come."

I smiled and asked, "Are you in pain?"

He nodded, yes, and the pain was evident in his eyes. He held my hand, and we were quiet. It was the first time I felt worried about a male. It bothered me to see his pain and to imagine that he had been stabbed. I stayed briefly at the hospital while worrying that someone would see me with him and tell Uncle Son. I knew that would result in me getting an unbelievably bad beating, which I just could not imagine living through. Len asked his friend to drive me home and made me promise that I would be there the next morning when he was scheduled for discharge.

The next morning his friend picked me up after I dropped my brother off at school, and we went to the hospital to pick up Len. Len told his friend that he wanted us to drive into Ocho Rios. He took me to an expensive local restaurant called *Ruins*, where he bought me lunch. That was my first time in a restaurant, and I ordered food and ate little since I was so nervous. A few weeks later, Len's bandage was removed, and he had a long knife scar from his eye to the middle of his cheekbone. Uncle Son, not knowing his story, would refer to Len as the "Bun up face bway" when he saw Len waving to me several times after this.

One day, I told Len, "I have to leave." I knew Len could not imagine the life I was living and my thoughts.

"You don't have fi leave. You can come and live with me. Your father could never touch yuh as long as yuh with mi," Len responded.

I imagined living with Len and of always hiding from Uncle Son. I knew that if I were with Len, I would be safe, but I also knew that I could not live with Len and be his "woman." I was not ready for that. I had dreams and goals and knew that agreeing to such a life would limit me. I did not want to have many children like Dahlia.

"Mi can't do that," I muttered.

"Where yuh plan to go?" he asked.

"To New York, to Buku's mother," I told him.

He looked relieved. His light brown eyes stared back at me before they were filled with tears.

"If you need anything, let me know," he said.

A few weeks later, Camille H., and I sat in Len's car as we said our goodbyes at Old Road. "I love you," he mumbled as he pulled me towards him.

I let him hug me as he rubbed my head. I cried because I knew I did not know where I was going or what I was doing. As he held me, I knew I was walking away from a man who had been kind to me and who viewed me as a good person.

"Be good always, and don't make no man spoil you," Len said.

Len held my face with his hands and held my chin as he stared into my eyes. "Mi know yuh afraid, but no one will ever hurt yuh. Don't let no man spoil yuh," he repeated as he hugged me.

I had no idea what that meant, but I responded, "Okay." That was our goodbye.

"Yuh no want to be involve with them people deh," Jeff repeated. It seemed that he noticed I was not focused on him. He was concerned about me, I thought. As he left for work, he hugged and squeezed me real hard against him. I was uncomfortable with his hug, and I remained immobile.

Once Jeff left for work, I walked around the apartment and stared out the window down to the street below. It was my first time being in an apartment building, and there was not much to see, only the back of another building. I washed the dishes and cleaned the apartment.

A few weeks later, I started working as a live-in babysitter in Long Island with a Jewish family that had two daughters. Lea had gotten the job for me. The wife was a social worker, and the husband was a painter. I was given my own bedroom, and it was my responsibility to care for their two girls, Rachel, and Beth. Jeff called me daily and talked to me, and one day, as he got off the telephone, he said, "I love you." I believed him, and I was gullible. I did not question his motives. "Lea is moving out," he told me another day, as he described all the problems they were having in their relationship.

One weekend, I went there, and Lea was gone. I was nervous knowing that Jeff and I were alone. I was sitting in the living room on the couch, and he came and sat next to me and started kissing me and touching me. I realized that he expected sex from me. For the first time in my life,

I consented to have sex with a man. I was disconnected from the act of sex. My view on sex was that it was expected from me, and there was no pleasure in it for me. I stayed awake for a while, disappointed with life. That night Uncle Son chased me in my dreams while I searched frantically for my lost passport.

Several days later, Jeff's father called and told him that his mother was ill and that his mother was angry with him for being with me. Jeff informed me that he was traveling to Jamaica to visit her. I returned to work in Long Island while Jeff traveled to Jamaica. Jeff called me from Florida on his return trip from Jamaica and told me he was visiting his friend Dara. Dara was from Brown's Town; I knew her and her family.

"And I have to ask you something when I return," Jeff said. I suspected Jeff's question would be on my abuse, which I was certain that J. must have told him. I wished I were dead. I had tried killing myself twice before. The first time was when I was fourteen years old. I drank alcohol and took all the pills I could find before going to sleep. I do not know if it was a hallucination, but I felt as though I was awakened by a "shadow." I felt a hand pushing against my abdomen while the "shadow" hugged me. That hug was filled with warmth, and I found myself thinking of love, and a vision of a place that I knew was in America. As I lost myself in the warmth of the hug, I was filled with thoughts of God as I drifted back to sleep. The next morning, I woke up knowing that all would be well with me.

My second suicide attempt was when I was sixteen years old after Dahlia sent me back to Uncle Son's house.

That time, I took my brother's asthma medication and other pills I found in the home. That resulted in me vomiting for about a day until Ms. Lupin took me to Alexandria hospital. I sat there and thought the doctor was stupid not to know what I had done.

It was good that I was at work with the small children because I had no time to plan my death that day or that whole week. As the weekend got closer, I was afraid of seeing Jeff and hearing his question. That weekend, Jeff told me, "Mi know u was being abuse that's why you left Jamaica."

I was filled with shame, disgust at myself, embarrassment, and was unable to make eye contact with him. I wanted to die, and I promised that I would never tell any man about the abuse. I knew that only someone who had experienced abuse would understand the ability of an abused person to separate their self from abuse. Years later, I learned that I used disassociation to cope with the abuse. How do I explain that I had grown to hate my body for being female since my conclusion was that my body made me a victim? I went to the sofa and fell asleep there. In the morning, Jeff made no mention of the incident.

Chapter Four

Several weeks later, I started feeling weird. Although I had never been pregnant, I knew I was. I was seventeen years and eight months old, and the idea of a child growing in me was interesting.

Over the years, when Ms. Lupin traveled to the United States for months and left her three children under the age of ten in the home, I had been the principal caretaker since Annmarie rarely assisted with the children's care. All the helpers that Ms. Lupin hired to assist with the children's care never stayed because Uncle Son terminated them when they refused his sexual advances.

"I don't want a child," Jeff said.

"What?" I asked as I stared at Jeff.

"The baby, I don't want a child. You need to have an abortion." Jeff pointed at my belly.

"An abortion?" I asked. I had no concept of how an abortion was done and only knew the word because of the stigma attached to it in Jamaica. There were young girls who people whispered about who had abortions. They referred to them as "cemetery." Songs were even made to describe this act of killing a child. I was frightened about having an abortion, and I responded, "I cannot have an abortion. I cannot kill a life within me."

Jeff stared at me with his lips pouted out. His anger was evident in his eyes.

A few weeks later, I had a miscarriage, and I was happy when it happened. Jeff had to sign the hospital discharge papers when I was released from the hospital because I was underage. After the miscarriage, I did not return to work in Long Island because I was too embarrassed about being pregnant and worried about the family's perception of me.

I was by then an illegal alien; I had overstayed in the United States and was worried about being picked up by Immigration authorities and of being deported. Now my nightly dreams were of deportation and Uncle Son chasing me.

By the end of June 1987, Jeff was spending most of his time with his friend, Dara, who had now moved to Brooklyn from Florida. Jeff also spent his time at the horse race tracks or at the off-track betting shops where he spent most of his money. Since I had never been exposed to gambling, I did not realize he was addicted to gambling. Jeff had problems with paying the rent due to his gambling. He informed me that he would be moving to share an apartment with his friend, Michael, who had a two-bedroom apartment on Nostrand Ave and Avenue J. We moved into Michael's apartment, and after the move,

Jeff continued to stay out most of the time. One night, I watched from the window as Dara's car dropped him off at about six a.m. in the morning.

"I was playing dominoes with my friends," Jeff said when he came into the apartment and saw that I was awake. I was suspicious that Jeff was having sex with Dara. But since Jeff continued to say, "I love you" and was having sex with me, I equated sex with love. Around that time, I also noticed that I vomited when I smelled cigarettes and Chinese food. I suspected that I was pregnant again.

One Sunday morning, shortly after Jeff arrived home, the doorbell rang. When I answered it, Dara and her mother stood at the door. Dara walked into the apartment, and I saw that Jeff appeared uncomfortable and anxious. Dara was one of the older girls that had loved to pull out my long braids while I was a student at Brown's Town Primary School and combed my hair. Dara was several years my senior, and I thought of her as being beautiful. I never imagined that we would be with the same man.

"Maxine, you need to find another place to live so Jeff and I can have our life together." I stared at Dara as I realized Jeff had been lying to me. "I'm pregnant, and you need to move soon," Dara continued.

I stared at Dara and her mother. Dara's mother was about ten times my size, and Dara was twice my size. I had never felt vindictive before, but I wanted to hurt Dara and hurt Jeff.

"Did Jeff tell you I'm pregnant too?" I said calmly.

Dara's face looked as if it were about to explode, and I was pleased. "Jeff said he's only helping you because he's sorry for you. I only come to New York so me and Jeff can make a life together. He said you was sleeping on the couch, and that he felt sorry for you," Dara said tearfully.

She looked at Jeff as she cried, "How can you do this to me, Jeff? Mi even send Debbie back to Florida because you and she was getting close." Debbie P. was another student from Westwood High School that Dara had brought with her to New York. She looked at me pityingly while I glared at her.

Dara was crying loudly as her mother held onto her and escorted her from the apartment.

I was so angry that Jeff had told her my story. I found myself thinking as I watched Dara and her mother leave the apartment. They were both angry at Jeff for telling lies, and I was pleased that I told them and caused misery to both.

"What did you tell them that for?" Jeff glared at me as he walked towards me and slapped me across my face.

I ran past the dining room table, grabbed the frying pan, and used all my strength channeled by anger to hit Jeff in the head. I was no longer in the present. I was reflecting on Diane using me as a shield when I was younger to block her husband's punches. I had taken Uncle Son's beatings, but I had no intention of taking another man's beatings. Jeff looked at me in pain and surprise as the frying pan connected with his head. I felt no empathy, only anger, and a sense of destruction. A few days later, Jeff informed me he planned on moving to Connecticut, where Lea was now living.

I was about four months pregnant in the fall of 1987

when Jeff moved to Hartford, Connecticut. Jeff asked his Aunt Yvonnie for me to stay with her. Aunt Yvonnie and her daughters Cynthe, Pauline, and Annie were from England and spoke with a British accent. Their house was located on Sterling Street in Hartford. I went to live with them while Jeff went to live with Lea.

Jeff rarely visited me or gave me money for food, so when Cynthe asked me to babysit her five-year-old daughter Charlene while she was at work, I agreed. I figured that was my way of earning my stay in their home. I was nauseated and vomited multiple times throughout the day, and Annie told me I needed prenatal care. She told me how to register at the local hospital for prenatal care. The clinic placed me on high risk due to my low weight, and I was given Ensure to drink daily.

I cried and prayed daily for a healthy child while my weight fluctuated. I did not like being pregnant. I read books on pregnancy, but nothing prepared me for the pain of childbirth. I gave birth to a daughter in the spring of 1988. She had my hair but looked like Jeff. I stayed in the hospital for about three weeks after birth because I developed an infection due to some of the placenta being left in me.

During this time, Jeff's cousin, Annie, was nice to me and helped me through that period. Aunt Yvonne was quite open with her dislike and view of Jeff and told me repeatedly, "Jeff was spoiled and is not a good man." She also made me aware that he had impregnated another woman that was employed at the local nightclub. Jeff denied it, and it was not until about fourteen years later that I learned that the woman had a son for him shortly after Tijay's birth.

About four months after Tijays's birth, I asked Jeff to drive me back to New York because Pauline asked me to leave their home while Aunt Yvonne had started mentioning, "Some nice men from the night club that would be nice for me." I concluded that New York was best for me since I was able to walk to places, unlike Connecticut, where I needed a car. Since I was an illegal alien, I was ineligible to obtain a driver's license or get a decent job. I was officially navigating the United States as one of the millions of undocumented people that lived in the shadows in the United States.

In September of 1988, I was back in Brooklyn. Jeff asked his friend, Atrick, to have me live in a house on Kenilworth Place at Flatbush Junction. At that time, I did not know that the house was being used as a crack house. I only learned it when I saw Atrick and his friend cooking crack in the kitchen. Since I had no other place to go, I felt resigned to making the best of the situation.

My bedroom was at the front of the house and next to the front door. I shared the kitchen and the bathroom with the two other men that lived in the house. I stayed in the bedroom mostly, and as the only female that lived there, I kept the bathroom and kitchen clean. As I write of that period, I realized that God kept me safe from all harm because one of the men smoked crack daily while other drug users frequented the home.

I often socialized with Atrick's two girlfriends, Jon, and Jacklyn, that visited him at the house. One day, I held Tijay in my arms and was talking to Jon on the street in front of the house when Jacklyn drove up. She greeted me by saying, "Hey Maxine, a da gal Atrick with?" Jacklyn was out of the car in seconds and pounced on the surprised Jon. Jacklyn grabbed Jon by her hair while Jon was trying her best to fight back by pulling on Jacklyn's braids. I was unable to intervene and could only watch as they both fought over Atrick. Jon took a beating that day, and my conclusion was that it was shameless for women to fight over men. I promised myself to never fight over a man.

Towards the end of October 1988, I felt a sudden urge to dress Tijay and leave the house. When I returned to the house, it was boarded up, with police locks on the door. I was told by one of the neighbors that a woman had overdosed on the drugs she had bought from the house and that the police had raided the house. The only man who was present in the house at the time of the police raid was arrested.

With the house boarded up, I used to climb through the back of the house to access the bedroom to sleep with Tijay. I had no money for food, and I survived by eating at Jon's house when I could and by asking strangers (only women) for a token to travel on the bus to Jon's house. I also breast fed Tjay which often left me starving most of the times. Sometimes, Jon allowed me to sleep at her house, but since she lived with her mother and other relatives, her mother did not want anyone staying there.

On one of my visits to Jon's house, she introduced to me to her mother's tenant, Dexter. Dexter was from Trinidad and told me his fiancé was employed in Asbury Park, New Jersey. He said that if I were able to find childcare for Tijay, he would refer me to a job in New

Jersey. Jon also started giving me a bad attitude when I slept there. Sometimes Tijay would cry, and Jon would start sucking on her teeth. I realized that she invited us to her home because she knew if we were there, Jeff and Atrick would stop by.

One night, as I slept with Tijay in the house on Kenilworth Place, I was awakened by the sounds of one of the "crackhead man" trying to break the door down. I prayed so hard for protection, and when he finally went away, I decided not to sleep in the house again. The following three nights, I slept in Jeff's old car that he had parked on the street at Kenilworth Place.

The car was cold at night, and Tijay cried so hard I became worried that the "authorities would remove her from my care." Jon had told me that the "government took children away if parents could not care for them," and that frightened me. Jon told me to go and apply for welfare benefits, but my fear of government and deportation was greater than my basic needs, so I never applied for welfare benefits.

After the third night in the car, with Tijay screaming from the cold, I decided to telephone Jeff to come and take my daughter. I telephoned Lea's number, and Jeff answered. He agreed to come and take our daughter. The next morning, as I waited for Jeff's arrival from Connecticut, I believed I finally understood how Dahlia must have felt when she brought me as a baby and left me with my paternal grandmother. It occurred to me to contact Dahlia in the future. When Jeff came and took our daughter home to Lea, I knew Lea would take care of her while I got myself together, but I felt broken again.

The day Jeff took Tijay, I contacted Dexter and informed him I was ready to go to Asbury Park. Dexter agreed to escort me on the bus from the Port Authority Terminal to Asbury Park, New Jersey. On the way there, Dexter told me, "Tony is going to fall in love with you."

"What are you talking about?" I asked.

"You are pretty, Tony likes pretty women, and you are young and pretty."

I started worrying. I felt uncomfortable when men talked about me being beautiful. I could not turn back. I was "homeless." I finally knew the word that described me. The only difference between me and some of the homeless people was that my clothes were still clean, and I was not using drugs or alcohol.

"Don't look so scared. Tony is not a bad person," Dexter said.

We were silent the rest of the way there, both occupied with our own thoughts. Dexter and I arrived at Tony's house on Sunset Avenue, not far from the ocean, in the late afternoon. Dexter had apparently called Tony and told him to expect us because Tony opened the door of his white two-storied home and greeted us with smiles.

Tony appeared to be around forty years old, over six feet tall, and slender. Tony's face was also thin, and he wore his hair in Jerri curls. I thought he looked like a pimp from the old movies that I had seen on television. He invited us into his home to sit on his white leather sofa in his all-white living room before introducing me to Angel, his fourteen-year-old daughter. I observed Angel smiling at Tony while he playfully held her hand as she talked to him. I observed love between them and saw trust in her eyes as she looked at him. It occurred to me that Tony genuinely loved his daughter, and that Angel returned his love. So, I relaxed and told myself that he might not be a bad man.

"Have you ever worked?" Tony asked.

"No," I answered.

"Do you know how to mop and clean?" he asked.

"Yes," I answered.

"How old are you?" Tony asked.

"Nineteen," I responded.

"You look much younger than nineteen," Tony replied.

"I have a daughter that lives with her father," I told him.

"You will have to stay here for now. There is no room at the house." Tony told us.

"The house?" I looked at Dexter.

"The house on Bond Street. You will be fine. Tony will not hurt you." Dexter reassured me.

"I live here with Angel, and I won't bite you," Tony said laughingly.

Dexter said goodbye and left. That evening my breast was engorged, and I was in a lot of pain as the milk soaked through my shirt while I sat at the dinner table with Tony and Angel.

"Let us go get you some pads for your breast, girl," Tony said.

My face must have shown my embarrassment, to

which Tony said, "Look, girl, you have nothing that I have not seen before. So, put some shoes on, and let us go to the store."

I did as Tony instructed, and he took me to the drug store and bought me breast pads. He also stopped at the supermarket and told me to get the food items that I wanted. I did not get much because I was worried about him paying for the items and thanked him profusely for his actions.

My bedroom was next to Angel's bedroom, and that night I fell asleep after asking God to watch over Tijay. The next morning, I woke up to find Tony making breakfast for us. After breakfast, Tony drove me to the house on Bond Street and introduced me to everyone, including Jen, Dexter's sister who had just come over from Canada and the other workers who lived there. That night, Tony drove me to the office and introduced me to the other workers.

The workers from the United States were all substance users, I later learned, and the other workers were illegal aliens. They were from India, Bangladesh, Grenada, Trinidad, and Jamaica. Tony told the workers that no one should "Mess with me," and I became known as "Tony's woman," which probably kept me safe from some of the workers. It took a long time for my body to adjust to working from 10 p.m. at night to 7:00 a.m. in the morning doing janitorial work. It helped that some of the workers worked quickly once we arrived at the store, so we could sleep for several hours despite a "no sleeping" rule.

Our job was providing maintenance service in Consumer stores, Kmart stores, and Bradlees stores all over South Jersey. Most times, I was responsible for sweeping, cleaning the bathrooms, and mopping the store's smaller sections, while the men did the most difficult work. Waxing the floors was the most difficult part of the job, and it would take larger groups to go into the stores to do the job. Those were the rare times that Tony worked with the cleaning crews, and he would schedule me to work in the store he was working in. Tony often visited my assigned store some mornings and suggested I ride with him to the other stores while he performed store inspections.

During those trips, he played music of the 60s and 70s, which I grew to love. Tony was the first man I had ever known that opened and closed doors for females. The more Tony learned of my relationship with Jeff, the more he educated me about men. Tony told me, "Men should take care of their children." "A woman should never have to ask a man for money because real men knew to take care of their women." "Men have sexual needs and satisfying their needs did not mean love." He repeatedly told me that I was young and did not know anything about life, love, or sex, and I had no business having a child. That made me cry because I knew it was true.

There were days that Tony would take Angel and me to the mall. As he shopped for Angel, he told me to pick up things for myself too. Most times, I did not shop for myself. It was on one of those trips that Tony bought me my first piece of jewelry, a diamond ring that he told me to try on. Some weekends, I accompanied Tony to the casinos in Atlantic City, where the bright lights, restaurants, and social life were all new to me, and I liked it. Tony showed me how to throw the dice and had me roll the dice at the tables. He would happily split the money with me that I won for him. Tony often teased me by saying, "You are my lucky star." Tony also told me that Tijay could visit me at his house on the weekends that I did not have to work.

Several months later, I started feeling uncomfortable in Tony's presence after he tried to hold my hand when we were in his car on one of his weekly store visits. As I moved my hand quickly away from him, he commented, "You must a been through some real stuff. You moved like I was going to hurt you."

I stared at him and said nothing.

One day, while we were in the kitchen, Tony told me, "You are like a scared cat. You won't survive like that."

I stared at Tony and knew he was correct about me feeling scared. I was always scared about Uncle Son finding me and taking me home, and I was scared to sleep at night because I was plagued by nightmares.

Tony laughed loudly as he said, "One day."

"One day what, Tony?" I asked.

"You will learn that what I'm telling you is the truth," he said before he turned to the kitchen sink and started whistling one of his favorite songs.

As Christmas drew near, Tony started decorating his house for the holidays. Tony had a white Christmas tree in the living room next to the fireplace and a blue Christmas tree in the dining room next to the bar. He lit the fireplace as the days got colder, and I loved sitting in front of the fireplace listening to music with Angel.

For the first time in my life, my environment felt safe and peaceful. Although the nightmares about Uncle Son continued, it was no longer my first thought in the morning. A few weeks before Christmas, Tony was in the kitchen cooking, and as I walked past him, he reached out and grabbed my hand. I tried to pull away, but he held it and pulled me towards him.

I was terrified and started shaking. Tony held on to my arms and stared at me.

"I am sorry. I won't' hurt you. I will not hurt you," he repeated.

"You look so scared. Somebody must have done some real stuff to you." He let go of my arm and went and sat at the table.

"So, what happened? Is it the baby's father?" He asked.

"No, I don't want to talk, Tony," I said.

"What are you afraid of?" Tony asked as I went upstairs to the bedroom.

We were quiet at dinner that night as Angel talked about school. The next day I asked Tony to move to me the house on Bond Street, but he reiterated there were no rooms there. I knew our relationship was changing, and I questioned my feelings towards Tony. I liked him for all he did for me. However, I knew he was too old for me and that I could not love him the way I imagined loving someone to be. I only felt empty and hollow on the inside. I was learning to accept what life was giving me. It could have been anyone that was being kind to me. I would have felt the same. I felt gratitude and nothing else. I had an empty feeling that I knew I had to resolve before I settled anywhere. I knew that I was just beginning life's journey, and Tony was not the end of that journey.

A few days before Christmas 1988, Tony was standing downstairs, and as I walked by, he pulled me towards him with a hug. Tony hugged me, and I did not hug back. It occurred to me that I needed hugs and a good cry. I felt emotionally exhausted and tired, and I let him hold me while I cried. Tony held me while rubbing my head and once I was done crying, I pulled away from him. He said nothing as he put his favorite music on.

The next day, when I arrived home in the morning from work, I found a Caucasian woman in the kitchen wearing Tony's robe. It was his girlfriend that had decided to visit him. Tony spent most of the day on the couch, flipping the television channel quietly. That night as he drove me to work, Tony was quiet before he muttered, "I did not tell her to come."

"That is your business. It has nothing to do with me," I said. "I'm not staying there."

"Why not? It is my house. She can never tell me who stays in my house," he responded.

"I do not want to stay there," I repeated.

Tony was silent before he told me, "I really don't want you in that house on Bond Street. Jack is a vulture." Jack was the owner of the house.

"I don't care," I responded.

"If that is what you want to do, then I won't stop you," Tony said. "But don't forget you are mine."

"Yours? I don't belong to anyone," I responded.

Tony laughed as he responded, "You belong to me. You just don't know it yet."

Chapter Five

The next day, I moved to Bond Street. The house's location was picturesque as it was located across from a lake that had ducks living on it. The inside of the house was drab compared to its beautiful location, and it was furnished sparingly. My bedroom was on the third floor at the top of the stairs, and there were two beds in the room and a dresser. Pat, a female, occupied one bed, and the other was mine. Pat would later tell me that she had been a nurse prior to drugs controlling her life. Pat was later terminated, and after Pat left, Jen, Dexter's sister, who was a few months older than I was started sharing the room.

Jen was dark-chocolate colored, with beautiful black eyes, a Coca-Cola® bottle shape, a big butt that I could never have, and a beautiful smile. Jen and I immediately connected and started sharing stories about our country of origin. Jen was from Trinidad and told me all about Trinidad. We eventually started working in some stores together at night as our friendship grew, and Jen often teased me about Tony being in love with me and about Tony's "crusty feet." Tony continued to show up on Bond Street every weekend and brought me groceries and any other items that he thought I needed. He would also give me money, which I often refused, but he would not leave until I took it.

I viewed Tony as a good person, although I was conscious that he wanted me to be his side woman. The truth was that it had become important for me to think that there were good people around because it took a great deal of energy and effort for me to see good in people. My short experiences in life by then had taught me nothing but pain. I did not trust any man. I did not have anyone. I was alone and needed to survive. Tony had shown me kindness without knowing me. He had welcomed me, a stranger, into his house. I knew where Tony kept his money and his jewelry, and Tony had created an environment for me to feel welcome, and I was grateful for that. I knew if I started believing that all people were bad, I would lose hope in life and living.

As we shared stories, I listened in awe as Jen told me of her experiences. For the first time in my life, I found someone with whom I could share specific events. We cried as we talked, and it was interesting for me to learn that although we lived in different countries, abuse was just as common in other countries. I could tell Jen things I never imagined I could speak of as I grew to value her friendship and knew it was the beginning of a lifetime friendship. Talking to Jen was the beginning of my road to healing. We both had our idea of punishment for child molesters and would often be very descriptive of what we would do to them if we could. Jen used to say, "Maxine, you are beautiful. You do not even know what people see when they look at you. You have to wear nice clothes." She gave me some of her dresses to wear. Jen's dresses were sexy, but they were form-fitting and showed all the curves of my body.

One day, Jen bought a Ouija board from Kmart, and we sat at the kitchen table and started talking to the board. We were both shocked when the pieces started moving to answer the question that we asked. As the piece moved, Ken, one of our co-workers, walked into the kitchen and admonished us about "opening the doors to spirits." We were scared and hid the board in the closet. Jen and I often traveled to New York by bus on our days off, where she visited her mother and shopped for clothes. Sometimes we just walked around and looked at all the items displayed in the expensive stores that we thought we would never be able to afford. Jen and I became inseparable, and Tony started teasing me by asking me, "What are you and Jen doing in that room all the time?" Sadly, Jen decided to return to New York to live with her mother and invited me to stay with her. However, Jen's mother told her she did not want me in her home.

As I continued to work and live on Bond Street, I made friends with some of the other women in the house. One Saturday night, I sat in Mag's apartment on the first floor. Mag was one of the females from Trinidad and would later become Tony's best friend, Keith's wife. As I talked to Mag and her niece Carol, I observed Carol nodding off. When I tried to talk to her, she appeared disoriented. I then realized that she had swallowed a bottle of pills that she had been holding in her hand. I screamed for Mag to call 911. Carol was taken to the hospital, and I observed as they flushed her system from her attempted suicide. That was a frightening experience, and I felt empathy for her as a woman. I also decided that I would not attempt suicide by overdose as I watched the doctors insert tubes in her to induce vomiting.

Some Saturdays, one of my co-workers, Leon would become intoxicated and stand outside the house yelling, "Maxine, I love you. Get rid of Tony and come to me." Someone must have told Tony that was happening because one Saturday, Tony showed up at the house. He went to Leon and told him to stop doing that. Leon was heard screaming at Tony, "I want your woman, Tony." Tony spoke to Leon calmly and politely as he encouraged Leon to go home and sleep. That day, Tony told me that I looked like Leon's wife, who had died several years earlier. Sadly, Leon fell in the lake one day while he was intoxicated and died.

I spaced out a lot during those years. I had a roof over my head and food to eat, but I felt detached when I was alone. I felt as though there was more, I should be doing, but I did not know where to begin. I looked at everyone around me and saw that I was the youngest person that lived in the house and worked at the cleaning company. I knew everyone had a story, and when I worked with some of my coworkers, I talked to them about themselves and their families.

I liked Camille, who was once a registered nurse. She told me of loving the wrong man that "turned her onto drugs" and of having lost her nursing licenses due to her drug use. There was Shivon, one female who knew all Whitney Houston's songs whose only desire in life was to meet Whitney. I liked the Trinidadian women, who worked daily to support their families and build their homes in Trinidad. I did not work every day since Tony insisted that it was hard work and that I needed to work no more than four days per week, even at times when I insisted that I wanted to work more hours.

I knew the men that insisted on being paid daily to support their drug habit and borrowed money weekly from Tony till their next payday. I empathized with Ken, the drummer that was kicked out of a famous music group. I observed workers steal by using the mop or the broom to knock cigarettes or snack items off the store shelves, then sweep the items all the way to the back of the store to where the garbage cans were located before picking up the items and putting it in their pockets.

I learned to be cautious of the workers that spent a long time in the bathrooms at nights, only to be observed coming out of the bathrooms drenched with perspiration and telling me to "Just clean the bathrooms," while they mopped the entire store by themselves with high energy because they had been using drugs in the bathroom.

My co-workers were unhappy, and that showed on their faces as they rarely smiled or laughed. It was as if "victim" was invisibly stamped on their foreheads. I was curious about their lives, and as I listened to their stories, I became aware that there were other issues in life apart from sexual abuse. There were drug and alcohol addictions, prostitution, poverty, homelessness, immigration issues, and lack of a support system.

Frequently, I thought of religion as I saw the despair that surrounded me, and I could not help thinking that my life mirrored most of the people around me lives. For the first time, I learned that people coped differently when life has been harsh to them. Drugs and alcohol were commonly used around me as a means of coping, while others like me were focused on religion, namely God, to motivate us and give us hope for a future. I prayed daily and bought my first Bible, which I spent time reading while memorizing specific Bible passages, which I repeated on the days when it was difficult for me to think beyond the hurt and shame with which I struggled.

My favorite Bible verse was in Psalm 91.

Psalm 91:1-7

1 Whoever dwells in the shelter of the Highest will rest in the shadow of the Almighty.

2 I will say of the LORD, "He is my refuge and my fortress, my God, in whom I trust."

3 Surely, he will save you from the fowler's snare and from the deadly pestilence.

4 He will cover you with his feathers, and under his wings you will find refuge; his faithfulness will be your shield and rampart.

5 You will not fear the terror of night, nor the arrow that flies by day,

6 nor the pestilence that stalks in the darkness, nor the plague that destroys at midday.

7 A thousand may fall at your side, ten thousand at your right hand, but it will not come near you.

That psalm gave me a feeling of peace when I said it.

The people around me were all "broken mentally," and I often wished there was a way to "help everyone" and to improve our lives. We were at the bottom, way down at the bottom of society, and it would take determination to pull us up. Camille often said to me when we worked together, "You are too young to be here. Look around you. This is not where you want to be or end up."

I knew she was correct. I told myself I would work on doing good things with my life and not go through life without a smile. I promised that I would listen to others, provide comfort when I could, and smile my way through whatever struggles that life would bring me. I knew that smiling would not make me ever appear to be a victim because I did not want to be viewed as a victim.

1989 was the year the Berlin Wall fell and was the year Dexter got married at Tony's house. Tony's girlfriend was absent from the house that weekend, and I had Tijay with me at the wedding. Tijay needed diapers, and I asked Tony several times to drive me to the store to purchase diapers, and he kept saying, "I'm coming. I'm coming," as he returned to socializing with some women next to him on the sofa.

I waited for about an hour, and Tony did not move from the couch. Fida, a Jordanian male who was about two years older than I was, overheard when I asked Tony about going to the store, so he said to me, "I am going to the store. I can drive you there."

I accepted his offer, and on returning to the house, I went upstairs to use the bathroom. As I exited the bathroom, Tony walked up to me and punched me in my stomach. Then, he walked quickly back down the stairs.

I was gasping for breath as I ran downstairs, filled with rage and thoughts of hurting Tony. Tony had returned to sitting, laughing, and talking to the females as if nothing had happened. I ran to the bar, grabbed a bottle, and ran towards him. Tony's best friend, Keith, ran and grabbed my arms while Tony was staring at me, angry and shocked.

"I am going to hurt you, Tony," I repeatedly screamed as Keith pushed me out of the house and drove me home. I cried all the way there while I explained to Keith that Tony had punched me in the stomach. Others that were present that day believed I attacked Tony because I was jealous.

That week, I ignored Tony when I went to the office, and Tony punished me by assigning me as one of the last people to work while he repeatedly stared at me for a reaction. After about two weeks, he showed up at the house and asked to speak to me, "What do you want, Tony?" I asked him.

"I just saw red when you left with Fida," Tony said.

"What, you have your woman, Tony. You want to have two women, a black one and a white one?" I asked him angrily.

Tony stared at me before answering, "You don't even see how I feel about you."

"Really, Tony. You want me to be the black one?" I said angrily. "I'm sure you will not hit her, but you want to hit me. Leave me alone Tony."

"I am sorry. I will not hit you again. I promise you," Tony said.

I believed him until about two weeks later. I had gone

to a co-worker's birthday party with Mag, and Tony was there. He offered to drive me home when I was ready to leave since Mag was not ready. On arriving home, I opened the door and saw that Jen was there with a male, and I closed the door. Tony walked out angrily and drove off. About an hour later, I heard him calling me. As I approached the car, Tony's fist flew out the window and connected to my cheekbone. I was too shocked to react and held onto my face as I watched him drive away.

The next day, my face was bruised and swollen. Jen tended to my face before returning to New York and showed displeasure at the sight of the bruise. "Max, what gives Tony the right to hit you? Do not have any man hitting you. Does Tony think he owns you?" Jen said.

I looked at Jen, thinking that Tony owned me. For the past year that I had lived in Asbury Park, Tony had provided for me financially. I never had to ask him for anything. He would just give me money and anything that he thought I needed. It was my fault that he was hitting me, and I deserved it. As I internalized Tony's behaviors, I made a promise that no man would ever have that power over me financially again.

Later that day, Mag saw the bruise on my face and said, "Keith said he has known Tony for all his whole life and has never seen Tony hit a woman or behave that way, Max. Keith said he does not know the reason that Tony behaves that way towards you."

I stared at her as I wondered why men mistreated me, my early life of molestation, my involvement with Jeff, and of being hit, first by Jeff, and now Tony. For the first time in my life, it occurred to me that I was vulnerable, and that Tony was right about me not knowing anything about life. I made a promise to myself to toughen up and to always keep moving before I got hurt again by any man.

The next day Tony showed up at the house. "I stopped by to see you," he said.

I turned my cheek towards him, and said, "Look at what you did to my face!"

"I am so sorry," Tony said.

"Leave me alone, Tony. You will never hit me again!" I screamed.

"You will never find someone who will look out for you," Tony told me. "How are you going to manage, you are young. You will never come off to anything," Tony said. I heard Uncle Son and Ms. Lupin's words in Tony's mouth.

"I don't plan to clean floors for the rest of my life!" I told Tony.

"What are you going to do? You are young and beautiful. Men will use you and spit you out." Tony yelled at me.

"Of course, you don't want me to leave. You want me to be around you, so you can beat me. I'm sure you would never hit your white woman." I screamed.

Tony's expression showed shock. "You are crazy," Tony said.

"Yes, I am crazy," I yelled.

Tony was quiet before asking, "Where do you plan to go?"

"New York," I screamed.

"If you do go, just remember you can always come back. You have a home here if you ever need one. If you need me, just call. Do you need any money?"

"I don't need your money, Tony," I screamed. Tony looked at me, took money out of his pocket, before turning all his pockets out as he said, "See, this is all the money in my pocket. I am giving it to you." He placed it on the dresser and walked out.

I picked up the money after he left because I knew I would need it later. It was $400.00.

I spent my last night on Bond Street after calling Shallo, my old friend from Westwood High School, asking to stay with her.

Chapter
Six

I packed all my clothes in my rolling bag and got on the New Jersey Transit Train, to the connecting train, to Plainfield, and to Shallo's apartment. I used to think of Shallo as a black Dolly Parton. Shallo had contacted me after arriving in New Jersey from Jamaica, and she was now living with her boyfriend, Fraggle, in a small studio apartment off Front Street. There was no room for another bed, so my bed was the blankets that I placed on the floor at night. It felt wonderful to have someone else there that I could talk to, although I still did not share my secret with Shallo.

Shallo offered to help me, and a few days later, she found me a job at the local diner in the evening. The owners were Greek, and the owner's wife stared at me repeatedly and kept telling me, "You are so pretty."

One night, as I wiped one of the tables, an attractive Hispanic police officer walked in and was observed talking to the owner's wife. She was smiling while they talked, and I noticed that he kept staring at me before he stopped their conversation and walked over to me and spoke. "Hi. My name is George. Where are you from, and what is your name?" he said.

"I am from Jamaica, and my name is Maxine," I answered. George was over six feet tall with light brown eyes. This was my first time to have a flirtatious conversation, and I smiled before responding.

"Maxine, that is a beautiful name," George said, smiling back.

"I know Jamaica. My ex-wife is from Jamaica," George continued.

"Really?" I said while I admired his long lashes and the toned body that was evident in his uniform.

"You have beautiful white teeth," George said as he leaned over the counter, smiling.

"Thank you." I smiled back.

George began stopping nightly on his tour. By then, he was only talking to me, and the owner's wife appeared upset while asking me nightly, "What does he say?"

"Nothing," I told her.

I told Shallo about George, and she started laughing. "He's the one that kissed my toes," she said. Shallo had shared that story with me before, and I was disappointed to learn it was George. So, the next night, I asked George, "Do you know Shallo?"

He appeared embarrassed. "How do you know her?" he asked me.

"She is my best friend," I answered.

"It does not matter. It's not like we are married," George said.

"No, we don't date our friend's ex-man," I said. George stopped coming to the diner, and the owner's wife fired me within a week of George no longer coming to the diner, which made me conclude that she was attracted to him.

Shallo often addressed my self-esteem issues by saying, "Maxine, you are such a pretty girl. You need to wear better fitting clothes."

I responded to her, "This is good," patting my clothes.

To which she responded, "Look at your face, your hair, your long lashes, show them girl. You are pretty, show them," with genuine admiration. "Let me dress you," she would say repeatedly. She did and bought me a black and white crotched dress that covered only my breasts, no coverage in my mid-section and barely covering my rear end, which I wore to a party and received many compliments from men and women about my figure.

Shallo and I often visited her mother, Ms. Pitchman, who was the only mother in our lives back then. Shallo and her mother had similar features. However, Ms. Pitchman was elegant in appearance, classy, and had a beautiful home. Ms. Pitchman encouraged us to believe in ourselves and work towards our personal goals. I enjoyed speaking with her while Shallo often teased me about her mother loving me because we had similar personalities.

Ms. Pitchman was always smiling, and I admired that, having been used to adults around me looking angry most of my childhood. Molly had also relocated to New Jersey and was living with her boyfriend, Trevor, in Newark. Molly was about six feet tall, of a medium complexion, had a pretty face, with shoulder-length hair, and always wore the latest designer clothes that accentuated her tiny waist and large hips. Molly often visited me when I was with Shallo, and they later became the best of friends.

On Saturday nights, Shallo, Molly, and I started hanging out at a Jamaican Club that was located on Front Street in Plainfield. We were later joined by Shallo's cousin, Michelle, and her friends, Aletta, and Peta. Aletta was petite, about my height, and an excellent reggae dancer. She drew attention from everyone when she danced.

I enjoyed being around Aletta because she was intelligent, had a great sense of humor, and we were comfortable together. Aletta would often tease me by calling me "Nurse Raddigan," as we shared beauty secrets. Molly and Michelle were our fashion designers and hairstylists. We did not have much money, but when we were together, we pooled our resources and helped each other. We were all illegal aliens, except for Peta, who worked in Medical Records at a local hospital. The rest of us worked jobs that paid little, and all of us had dreams and goals that were on hold until we got our green cards.

There was trust among us, and none of us could have predicted the betrayals that would later occur in our circle. Peta had sex with Trevor, Molly's boyfriend and Molly mailed a package to Aletta's home address that federal agents delivered. As a result, some relationships ended and strained the other existing relationships.

Retaining employment was difficult after I was terminated from the diner. I was hired and quickly terminated from a waitress job at another diner because I was never able to balance the plates. I was briefly employed in a women's clothing store on Front Street but was terminated due to poor sales. I found employment at a dry cleaners, where I learned to place the shirts on the steam pressing board. The owners were Koreans and were very patient with me as they taught me to press the shirts.

As I continued living with Shallo, she remained supportive. However, there was an issue of me waking up several times at night to find Fraggle walking around nude over me, so we decided it was time to move to a bigger apartment. We moved to Peta's father's house that had several vacant bedrooms off Front Street for cheap rent. I had my own room there because I was finally able to pay my own rent, and we ignored that our noses and clothes became filled with soot from the vents in the house.

Dread, Peta's brother, so named because of his long dreadlocks, also lived in the house with his girlfriend on the top floor. Dread traveled to Manhattan, where he bought cocaine wholesale. Shortly after I moved into the house, Dread approached me, "I need yuh to do something for me."

"What?" I asked.

"Can you go with me to Uptown with me, so I don't get noticed. Mi will pay you about $150.00."

"Really?" I asked. That was way more than the weekly salary I was being paid at the dry cleaners. "Okay." I agreed to accompany him to uptown Manhattan, ignorant of the risks I was taking.

I traveled with Dread to Washington Heights by subway to one of those vacant buildings. There were lightbulbs hanging from electrical wires all the way up the stairs to one of the higher floors where the Columbian drug dealers sold cocaine. The stairs and the room were manned by men with machine guns. I stood next to Dread in front of the glass table where an obese man sat with the cocaine, scales, and guns. I watched as Dread ordered his cocaine, watched it being weighed. Then, Dread paid for it and handed me the cocaine. I looked at him questioningly.

"Just put it in your boots," he said, beckoning to my knee-length winter boots.

I paused before putting it in my boots as instructed, thinking this was not part of the plan.

"Everything good, man," he reassured me.

We then walked back to the subway and traveled to downtown Manhattan where I handed Dread the cocaine. Then, I waited at an all-night diner while Dread disappeared in the vicinity of Washington Square Park.

One night, as I traveled uptown on the # 3 train with Dread, I observed the Police Canine Unit getting off the train. It occurred to me then I could get caught carrying cocaine. I was then aware of the drug laws by listening to the radio, and although I did not understand the specifics, I knew the consequence was jail time if I ever got caught. Later that night, I asked Dread, "I'm wondering what would happen if I get caught."

"Don't worry, mi wi tell dem it's mine," Dread responded.

"Yeah," I answered with disbelief.

"Yeah, man, nothing wi happen to you," Dread reassured me with a smile.

I told Shallo of my concerns, and she responded, "Max, you really believe that he would do that?'

"No," I said. The answer did not take much thought. I also was becoming disgruntled as I realized that Dread had purchased a new SAAB car, and he and his girlfriend were always shopping, while he was slow in paying me the agreed amount.

"I am not going with you anymore," I told Dread.

"You don't have nothing to be scared about," Dread repeated.

"I'm good," I said and walked off.

My mind was made up and I stopped going with Dread because I knew that I did not come all the way to be in America to be imprisoned. A few weeks later, Dread was arrested and sentenced to over ten years in prison. Once again, God showed me mercy, and I also knew it was time to leave New Jersey. I called Jen, who had her own furnished room in Brooklyn, and I moved back to Brooklyn.

Chapter
Seven

Moving in to share Jen's room was comforting as we reconnected. I found employment at Shoe Closet, a shoe store on Flatbush Avenue, opposite Erasmus High School, where I made the minimum wage of $3.75 an hour due to my immigration status. Jen and I split the rent and shared the household chores due to our likes. I loved to clean while Jen loved to cook.

After we paid rent and bought tokens to travel to work, we did not have money left for food, so we ate a lot of Chinese food as well as I accompanied Jen on her dates to eat. Molly also gave me money when she could and spent a lot of energy trying to get me "hooked up" with Trevor's friend Snogga.

Snogga was about 30 years old, a decade older than I was at that time. Snogga had cataracts in one eye, but Molly kept telling me, "Snogga is a good man. He can provide for you."

I talked to Snogga when I visited Molly, and Snogga talked about a girlfriend in Jamaica that he sent money to regularly. I never felt comfortable around Snogga and told Molly, "There is something about him I don't like."

Snogga telephoned me repeatedly, and Molly repeatedly told me, "Snogga really likes you. You should talk to him."

"Something about him I don't like," I used to tell her.

Snogga also started showing up at my room unexpectedly, and that made me so angry that I would have a bad attitude around him when he insisted on spending the night with the excuse that it was too late to get back on the train. One day I answered my phone and heard Snogga on the telephone, "How u doing? he asked.

"I am pregnant," I told him.

"For whom?" he asked.

"Mi baby father," I lied. I was not pregnant, but I told him that so he would stop calling.

He never called back. A year and a half later, Molly called and told me, "It's a good thing you never talk to Snogga."

"Really," I said, remembering all the times she tried to convince me to talk to Snogga.

"Snogga killed his woman," she said.

"Thank God, it was not you. He cut her up in pieces," she told me.

I whispered a prayer, thanking God it was not me and that I had followed my instinct to not have a relationship with him.

In the early 1990s, it was a constant struggle for me to pay rent, to keep a roof over my head, and to feed myself. At times, I felt I was ready to provide for Tijay but had to return her to Jeff and Lea because once I had her in my care, I realized I did not make enough money to pay for childcare and feed her. I was forced to accept that Jeff and Lea were able to provide for her and felt I was doing the best for Tijay by having her remain in their care.

I realized I had to obtain an education and work towards having a permanent home before having her live with me. Jen, Molly, and Shallo did not have children to care for and helped me sometimes but since we were all navigating life as "illegal aliens", our employment and salary were unpredictable.

I found comfort in praying, and when I was alone, I continued to meditate on the Bible and religion and wanted to feel God's presence. I visited various Christian churches in search of God's presence, and I even visited a mosque to hear their ideas on religion.

The more I learned about God, the more I struggled with some of the Bible teachings. There were so many Bible passages on forgiveness, and I could not imagine forgiving Uncle Son for what he did to me. I wanted him to apologize for all the hurt he caused in my life and for the person I had become.

There was one church I attended frequently, and on one of my visits to the church, I asked one of the church ministers about not being able to forgive someone. The church minister told me that if I did not forgive, I would go to hell. I stopped going to that church because I was filled with hate and anger and was unable to function in relationships. I stayed single most of the time.

One day, Molly told me, "Mi know a man who want to meet you?"

"Who?" I asked, remembering Snogga.

"Someone saw you and likes you. He is a good guy," she told me.

"You and your good guys," I laughed.

"No, man, this one is a good one. He has a good family. You should meet him," Molly said.

"Okay," I agreed to meet him.

I met Andy that weekend in New Jersey. Andy was of a dark complexion, over six feet tall, and athletically built from playing soccer. Andy lived with his family in New Brunswick, was enrolled in college, and worked part-time. I felt the animosity from Andy's family when I informed them that I was a mother and where I worked.

Andy rarely smiled and never initiated any activity, so we spent most of the time watching television, which I found boring. I viewed Andy as having a protective life and felt he could not relate to my life. Andy knew I did not have my green card and surprised me about two months after we met by saying, "I can marry you."

"What do you mean?" I asked.

"I can marry you and file for you," Andy repeated.

"Are you sure?" I asked.

"Yes, I don't mind," Andy said.

"What are you expecting? I do not have any money," I said.

"I will do it for you. I don't expect anything," Andy replied.

We planned to marry within a month after establishing that it was "business."

The night before we got married, Jen and I went to the Q Club in Queens, I did not like going to night clubs because I found the music too loud, but she encouraged me to go with her. At the Q Club, a man approached me and asked, "Would you like to dance?"

"Yes," I answered. After the dance was over, and I went to the bathroom. I found him waiting for me outside the bathroom door with red roses.

"My name is Jay." Jay was of a fair complexion, 5ft 11 inches, muscular body with one gold tooth and dimples when he smiled. "Where do you live?" Jay asked.

"Brooklyn," I responded.

"Me too," he said.

At the end of the night, he offered to drive us home, which we accepted since it saved us cab fare once he showed us his identification.

The next morning Andy came to my house, and we traveled to City Hall and got married. After the marriage, Andy went home to New Jersey, and I returned home to my furnished room at Quincy Street, in the Bedford Stuyvesant section that I shared with Jen. Later that week, as I walked home, Jay drove up. Maybe he had been waiting to see me while I viewed it as coincidental.

"Hello," he greeted me.

"Hi, what are you doing around here?"

"Passing by," he responded.

"Would you like to hang out tomorrow?" he asked.

"Yes," I responded and provided him with my work address. The next day, he picked me up from work.

Our first date was bowling and watching the movie *Ghost.* Jay opened my car door and other doors for me. He appeared charming and had a sense of humor. That first date ended up turning into numerous dates since he was spontaneous and fun to be around. I had never been around someone like that before and grew to like him.

I also moved into my own furnished room at Clarendon Road and New York Avenue and felt hopeful about my future. I spent so much time with Jay that I no longer saw Andy and was not focused on the agreement I had with Andy to file for my green card.

About three months after I met Jay, the shoe store management changed, and one day as I left work, the new manager Uzi who had recently arrived from Israel, asked to check my purse when I was leaving work. I was very offended and showed him my purse and yelled, "All this time, I have worked here and never stole from Perry. Now, you come here and accuse me of stealing."

I could not help thinking that since Uzi had just arrived from Israel, his view of me as a black person must have been a negative one to assume, I was a thief. I was humiliated by Uzi for viewing me as a thief. Jay picked me up from work that day, and I explained that I had quit my job.

"How do you plan on paying your rent?" he asked.

"I had not even thought of that," I told him truthfully.

"You can live with me till you figure it out," he offered.

"Are you serious?" I asked.

"Yes," he said.

I enjoyed Jay's company and hearing him tell me that I could move in with him made me think that he loved me. Jay was twenty-three years old, and I was twenty-one years old.

Once I moved in with him, I learned that Jay, in addition to being employed by New York City, was a music producer for many rap groups including the Fat Boys, The Bad Boys, TKA, The Force MDS, Doug E. Fresh, Slick Rick, Mary Jane Girls, The System, LL Cool J, Remembering, The Artist, Fresh Gordy, Sandra Wilson, New Edition, among others. Jay also had rap beats that were being sampled by many artists and he often wrote his music in the music studio he had in the house so I learned to sleep through loud music. Maybe if I knew more about that lifestyle, I would have been prepared for that life.

Jay spent a lot of time at social events and parties "mingling," as he called it. I found it exhausting to be a part of those events when he invited me. I also realized that many females were attracted to him, and that bothered me.

Jay visited with his son in New Jersey on the weekends. I never suspected he was still in a relationship with the son's mother since I was living with him until, one day, I answered the house telephone. The son's mother was on the phone yelling and screaming at me that they were

91

engaged. The son's mother and her mother then showed up at the house to tell me that I was destroying their life. I stood and listened to them and watched as the son's mother attacked Jay. I felt he deserved it, and by then, I had become callous and was no longer surprised by anything that occurred in my life or that men did.

Jay left and took them home while I sat on the couch, trying to figure out what I was going to do. When Jay returned to the apartment, I was quiet, and he finally said, "You don't have to leave." I interpreted that as love, so I stayed. It was not long before I realized that Jay was messing with other women.

Jay was African American and took pride in his heritage. He would often have me accompany him to listen to well-known Black speakers throughout the city. I learned the history of Black America and developed a better understanding of their struggles in America. It was at those meetings that I was introduced to books that educated me about Black America. I realized that my view of America was different as I did not live the struggles of Black Americans.

Jay also introduced me to museums and other cultural experiences that New York had to offer. There was never a dull moment with Jay. As we approached a year of living together with numerous fights due to his infidelities, Jay and I talked about me "screwing up with Andy," and Jay agreed to marry me and file for my green card. I filed for a divorce from Andy and got married to Jay in the fall of 1992 at City Hall.

Life got worse after the marriage because Jay stayed out every weekend. There were times he would take the house keys as he left for the weekend, and I had to travel to New Jersey and stay with Molly and Shallo, who were now sharing an apartment together in Plainfield. I moved out several times from Jay's house but returned when he promised that he would change. Also, I felt an obligation to make the relationship work since he was filing for my green card.

A highlight of our relationship was that Jay liked going to church and it was one of my visits with him to his mother's old church that I gave my life to Christ. During the times that we were separated, I had relationships that I screwed up with my trust issues and feeling of obligation to Jay. There was one man in 1997 that I felt loved me and offered me an opportunity to start a new life with him in North Carolina. But I was so broken by then, I could not even imagine starting over anywhere, so that man got married to someone else.

Chapter Eight

The bad relationship I had with Jay left me in emotional turmoil, and I contacted Dahlia to establish a relationship with her. We talked several times, but my relationship developed more with my sister, Car, who was attending nursing school. I told Car about the molestation that I had endured, and she admitted that Dahlia and my maternal relatives believed I was lying. I learned Dahlia was seventeen years old and did not want another child when she became pregnant with me and that I had thrived within her despite her efforts to kill me.

Learning about my early life made me empathize with Dahlia, and I tried extremely hard to create a bond with her, but it seemed she was incapable of having a bond with me. I started feeling stressed, hopeless and I started questioning my sanity. I did not have sexual desires for anyone, and sometimes I questioned if I could remain in heterosexual relationships. I tolerated men, but I did not love any man enough not to walk away from him. I spent a lot of time plotting my next move, and those moves never involved a man at my side.

There were so many thoughts in my head then, my problems with Jay, my inability to be financially independent, and the volatile environment to which I was now exposing Tijay. The nightmares worsened, and I was too ashamed to talk about my feelings to anyone. So, I spent a lot of time sleeping.

My migraines increased, while my participation in daily life was done automatically. Shame and guilt of my abuse never escaped my thoughts, and I attended church more regularly to give me meaning in life.

I was a church hopper; I visited many churches searching for a feeling of peace. I started reading the Bible more and started praying more. Having religion in my life made me remain hopeful about my life. I learned more Bible verses, repeating them when I felt hopeless, while I continued to think on forgiveness and imagined Uncle Son asking for my forgiveness.

I was bitter about life and did not think positively of all the men that had come into my life. It was so easy to blame everyone for all that had gone wrong in my life, but I knew that I would lose faith in people and in life if I did. I forced myself to believe in the hope that things would work out and that I should set lifetime goals even though I had no idea how to achieve my goals.

On February 23, 1993, I was at 26 Federal Plaza and had just been approved for my work permit when I heard a loud boom. I would later learn that it was the sound of the first bombing of the World Trade Center. The approval of my work permit made me feel I could begin the pursuit of the American dream. I obtained my driver's license and found employment as a nurse's aide first, before eventually going to work in the shoe department at Sears and Roebuck Store in the Flatbush section of Brooklyn.

In 1998, once my permanent green card was granted, I obtained employment at YAI/NIPD as a Community Training Specialist, where I taught employment skills to individuals that had disabilities. That environment taught me to appreciate life and taught me patience. I traveled to Jamaica that year with the intent to visit Uncle Son and Ms. Lupin and to confront them about the abuse. However, when I saw them, I was too ashamed to talk about it. I visited Dahlia and gave her the pearl necklace and earrings that I feel mothers should own.

On my return to New York, my paternal cousin, Peter, contacted me while he was enrolled at Howard University and visited me during some of his holidays from school. As I listened to Peter talk about his goals of completing college and observing him with his friends, I realized that heading to college was possible. Peter encouraged me to apply for college. I applied to Mercy College only because the school had night classes and was accepted there, while Jay told me, "Having a college degree don't mean anything."

In 1999, I finally felt ready to file for a divorce. After the divorce, I moved to an apartment on Ocean Avenue in Brooklyn, and I felt hopeful about finding love. I dated a lawyer that was featured in *Essence Magazine* in an article about what men wanted in relationships briefly.

Unfortunately, my trust in others was non-existent by then, and I must have appeared weird to him because I had unexplainable dreams that were about his life that he had never shared with me.

In early 2000, I again traveled to Jamaica to visit Car, and we visited Dahlia's house. Dahlia was not there when we arrived, so I waited in one of the bedrooms. I stayed in the bedroom for half an hour to see if she would come to greet me, and she never did. I then went out and asked her the reason she did not come, to which she responded, "I have to cook Mr. (the name she called her man) ...soup."

"You have your man every day. You never see me," I said. "Why did you have me?' I asked.

"I have seven children, and I never killed any," she said proudly.

"That is the mistake you made. You should have aborted me. You can't even imagine how my life has been and the struggle I go through daily just to live with me," I said.

Dahlia remained silent as I left her home with Car. For years, when I visited my siblings in London, Dahlia would talk to them on the telephone in my presence and never talked to me. That year, I was forced to cut ties with J., whom I had always respected and admired after an incident with her much younger boyfriend. I stored her good deeds in my heart and realized that my journey had to continue without her. I once again spaced out as I focused on the things that I had control of in my life.

Chapter Nine

Like everyone else in America, 2001 was a very memorable year for me. It was my final year in college, and I saw the smoke of the World Trade Center buildings as they burned on September 11, 2001. I was stuck with my group from YAI/NIPD in the community from 9 a.m. when the first plane landed until about 5 p.m. in the evening. I stayed calm while I worked on getting each of them home and was later given a Recognition Award from YAI/NIPD for going above and beyond duty.

I also made an important decision that year to pursue social work as a career and applied to graduate programs. At the same time, Shallo gave me a platform to speak of child abuse in 2002 during her promotion of domestic violence and its impact on children after I finally disclosed my reasons for leaving Jamaica.

I graduated Magna Cum Laude with a Bachelor's Degree in Behavioral Science and a minor in Business

Management and I was accepted at S.U.N.Y Albany School of Social Work Master's Degree Program. I found an apartment in Albany in the Summer of 2002 and packed Tijay and my clothes in my Toyota 4 Runner and headed to Albany. I started classes in September 2002, and my future never appeared brighter as I settled down to classes.

In mid-September 2002, I received a telephone call that would forever change my view on life. The New York Police Department called and informed me that Jay was in the hospital. I drove all the way from Albany to Kings County Hospital in Brooklyn. On my arrival at the hospital, I saw Jay covered in blood and restrained to the bed. I was frightened for him, and since Jay still had me listed as his spouse, all decisions had to be made by me.

Jay's journey was a long, arduous one for the next several years that followed. I made the decision not to return to school and to assist him with whatever he was going through. Jays' story is his own, so I will not elaborate any further.

On my return to Brooklyn from Albany, I did not work for a while as I provided support to Jay. Once I found employment, it was as a case worker for Little Children Services, a preventive service agency that exposed me to the harsh realities of child abuse in New York. I made home visits to children that were in the foster care system and worked with the birth parents for reunification. Some of the cases were like my childhood, and I was passionate about listening to the children as well as ensuring the Foster homes were safe for them. I worked there for several months before going home and finding an eviction notice on the door informing me that the house that I had rented was in foreclosure.

I was worried and frustrated with life in general and felt relocation would be beneficial to me. I moved to Gloucester, Virginia, in 2003, a city I had come to know when I had visited Jay's sister there. I purchased a home there and rejoiced when I was able to put the key in the house that belonged to me.

Living in Virginia had its challenges and its blessings. It was my first time being exposed to open racism. Since I was employed as a case manager for individuals with disabilities, I interacted with people that were open with their biases. There were families that expressed they did not want to work with me because of my ethnicity, as well as one of my female bosses informed me when I advocated for the individuals that, "You have the northern attitude." I often visited the small stores on Main Street in Gloucester and was treated rudely by the store owners, and I was also warned to stay home when the white supremacists marched in Gloucester on Main Street while I lived there.

My blessings came from several women that God placed in my life at work. They were strong and beautiful and shared their history of abuse by relatives and boyfriends. They were Hispanic, Black, and Caucasian women, and I saw them living their lives with passion and empathy for others around them. I admired them as I listened to their stories and observed that they viewed life as survivors. I cried with them as I heard their stories as I subconsciously released most of my pain on my journey to healing.

One woman told me, "I know that you must have asked

God why you lived through abuse. But you should know that if you had not been through those things in your life, your journey would have been different, and how would you know to help people and understand their pain if you never experienced it?"

That woman gave me an answer to the question "Why me? that I had struggled with for so long. Another woman told me about her personal goal of always being a light in other people's lives even while she was struggling with cancer. I took all the positivity of those women and made those ideas my mantra for life unbeknownst to them.

In 2004, I visited Peter in Los Angeles for the first time. I fell in love with Los Angeles and met Peter's friend, K-Fresh, who would later become my friend and confidante. As much as I loved the house in Virginia, I did not like being around racism. The neighbors often called the police to make reports about my dogs. I felt annoyed with my coworkers, who were often talkative and filled with complaints but became subservient in the presence of the bosses. I grew to dislike the environment and made the decision to return to New York after a medical scare with Tijay.

I returned to New York in 2005 and worked as a family educator in a preventative program before going to work as a child protective specialist with New York City Children Services in May 2007. I was fueled with a passion and a goal to ensuring that all children I came in contact were safe. That same month, Molly died after being in a car accident and being on life support since February 2007. I had a rude awakening as I told one of my close friends about Molly's car accident and of her being on life support and that friend's response was, "What goes around, comes around. Look what Molly did to Aletta." That statement haunted me for years since it made me question the loyalty I had always felt towards my female friends.

Molly had often made me aware of her wishes of never being placed on life support and I shared that with Diane when Diane asked me. Interestingly, just before the car accident Molly had started talking to me about death and when I went to her apartment while she was on life support I saw that she was reading a book about life after death. After Molly's death, Diane asked me to buy the burial dress and I picked a beige formal dress.

At the funeral, I did not get to see her in the casket, and only as it was nailed shut did I realize that I would never see her again. As I screamed with pain, Peter, held me, knowing how much I loved her. A part of me died with her and I was later forced to terminate my relationship with her children due to my strained relationship with Diane. I need to share that Molly, Shallo and I had a "promise" that "anyone that died first had to return and tell the others what death is." A few months after Molly's death I had a dream where she told me, "I am not allowed to tell you what happens after death, but I am asking you to please pray for forgiveness every day before you go to sleep."

After Molly's death I struggled with keeping my mental health intact while I continued to be a support to Jay. Her death forced me into space out mode as I placed all my energy into my work at New York City Children Services (ACS) with a purpose to make a difference in children's lives. I shared my story of abuse only twice in my profession, once to a teenaged boy that I asked to trust me with his story, who told me, "There is no way you will understand what I'm going through, and no ACS worker ever helped me."

"Please give me a chance to help you," I said, giving him my cell phone number. "I was abused for years till I was sixteen old, and I was told I would never be anything. But I refused to believe it or let the abuse dictate my life," I told him.

The young man was in tears as he said, "You are always smiling. You look like you had a loving mother." That weekend he left me a message informing me that he planned to come to the office on Monday to speak to me about his problems, which he did. Years later, I was informed by a case worker that this young man had become an A-student, was still residing in the group home I had placed him in and had goals of going to college.

I also shared my story with a fifteen-year-old female who was thrown out of the home by her mother after she shared that the mother's boyfriend was sexually abusing her. This teenager had stopped going to school because she was angry with her mother. I shared my story with her and hoped that she would know that the only person she was hurting was herself by not learning.

In 2009, I enrolled at Yeshiva University while I worked full-time and studied part-time to obtain a Master of Science in Social Work. As I focused on school, my few relationships faded into the background since I was no longer able to hang out as my studies and internship took my time. K-Fresh and I reconnected and spent many hours talking on the phone and it helped me with processing my grief before I sought grief counseling.

In 2013, I started my journey of forgiveness with Niema's help. Niema was a woman I met while I worked on the Visiting Nurse Services Mobile Crisis Team. Niema was Muslim, and I learned the power of forgiveness from her. I shared my story of abuse with Niema, and she worked with me to address my hate. Niema and I laughed and cried together and, once again, I realized that God had placed her in my life so I could learn to understand the concept of forgiveness and forgive Uncle Son and to move on to the next part of my journey.

I first reached out to my siblings that I was raised with and apologized for not being in their lives. I also apologized to all the people that I felt I hurt, including calling Uncle Son in January 2014 and being able to tell him, "I am calling to tell you that I forgive you for all the abuse you put me through. I do hope that one day you will ask God for forgiveness too."

After that, I felt as if the world had lifted off my shoulders. I felt a freedom that I never imagined possible. I asked my mother's children to tell her that I forgave her since she never tried to talk to me. I would later learn "she thinks it is my fault" that I was abused. Ms. Lupin continues to tell everyone around her that I lied about the abuse, as well as that she "never know nothing" when I confronted her in December, 2019, via telephone.

I still find it difficult to maintain relationships, and I sometimes attract men with their own demons. In 2011, I was with my coworker, Ms. Laney, from New York City Children Services on a visit to an apartment building in the Bronx when I met the building's owner. He was an extremely attractive man who spent months trying to convince me to date him. He turned out to be mafia. I learned that only when I saw his photograph on the front page of the newspapers in 2011. The newspaper described horrible deeds that he was responsible for, as well as all the places that were mentioned in the newspaper, were all places that he had called me from within the months that I had known him. There was also a well-known music producer that I met and who stopped calling me because he was upset that "You don't make time for me."

From late 2011 to 2016, I practiced celibacy as well as focused on my relationship with God and my healing. In 2017, I decided to date, and I met a successful man that had no empathy towards the less fortunate and always argued with me about any compassion I showed towards others. He even expressed not supporting my career of working in mental health. He warned me that he would "sue me" if I ever mentioned him in my book. I am guessing that having a bottle of wine thrown above my head when I terminated the relationship is worth mentioning.

And, of course, I must mention my on/off relationship with someone that I loved because of his positive attitude and when I slept next to him, I did not have the nightmares that are a part of my life. Sadly, I realized that he too had his own struggles and that he loves his women young and big-bodied and I did not fit in any of his criteria.

I never knew if it was "luck" that I have met such interesting men or if it is that I am being tested. Maybe because Tony taught me at an early age that everything had a price, I always refused offers for homes or cars, but

I must admit that I have had some interesting dates and gifts. Sometimes I think for a quick second, "how dumb I have been" since I have been around men with "money" and would not have had to struggle financially if I had been a "taker."

I know that it takes a strong man to be in a relationship with me since I carry trauma along with a distrust towards others. I continue to pray that God will send such a man to me and to all the other women that are praying for men.

I know that mental illness is often caused by trauma, and I work with others, knowing that my journey could have ended up very differently. I believe that it has only been through God's grace and mercy that I have been able to function as an individual and not as a resident on a psychiatric unit. The nightmares continue and I have learned that the best way to cope with them is by limiting my contact with all parties related to my trauma. Dahlia admitted in 2019, two months before her death, that she could not remember that far back as to who my father really was. In a way, that knowledge has given me a different perspective on life. I can dream that if she had made a different choice, I could have had a different life.

Conclusion

Jeff died from cancer in 2010, and Lea and I were able to talk about the past and put aside our differences. Lea continues to be a support in my life and taught me that life is full of forgiveness and hope. I look at Lea as we both grow older and I am grateful that Jeff brought us together without ever knowing that we would still be here long after his death.

I work in the field of mental health and have been honored to be nominated Social Worker of the Year by New York City Health and Hospital in 2017, in Psychiatry. My clinical training has also given me the advantage of knowing my limitations.

My friends tell me that "it does not matter about my journey" because God knows the person that I would be. I tell my story hoping that it inspires someone out there who is struggling with abuse or poverty that hope is real, God is real, and prayer is real. I believe in God, the power of His love, mercies, grace, and faith.

Epilogue

L ife is unpredictable and can be rough. Using faith, prayer, and hope will get you through your darkest moments.

Use forgiveness to fix your hurts. It is not for the person that did you wrong. It is for yourself. Living a life with bitter thoughts and feelings kills slowly.

Be kind and compassionate to one another, forgiving each other, just as in Christ God forgave you.
Ephesians 4:32

About the Author

Marlene A. Sherwood Hickman was born in Jamaica and ran away from Jamaica at seventeen years old due to abuse. Marlene used her belief in God utilizing hope and faith through prayer to work through her personal challenges and achieve her goal of helping others.

Marlene has been involved in community projects of facilitating community workshops for families in Bronx, New York and utilizes social media platforms to educate on mental health in her "Positive Food for Our Mental Health Series" under her "Loosethebroken Movement." Marlene believes her greatest achievement in life is to be able to testify on God's grace and mercies.

Marlene is a graduate of Westwood High School, Jamaica.

Marlene has a Bachelor Degree in Behavioral Science, Mercy College New York. Marlene has a Master of Science Degree in Social Work, Yeshiva University.

Marlene is a Licensed Clinical Social Worker and Therapist. Marlene has held positions as S.I.F.I Instructor at New York University and Adjunct Professor at Long Island University Master of Social Work Program.

Marlene was awarded the New York Health City and Hospital Social Worker of The Year Award in Psychiatry in 2017.

Contact

For more information, you can contact Marlene Hickman at:

http://www.loosethebroken.com/

hickmanmarlene@yahoo.com

31177 US Highway 19 N,
Palm Harbor, Florida 34684

Made in the USA
Middletown, DE
12 June 2021

42001982R00076